PETER A. DAVID

Aurum
Press

CONTENTS

1 WHO ARE THE AVENGERS? 9

2 WHEN CAPTAIN AMERICA THROWS HIS MIGHTY SHIELD 33

3 BEHOLD IN BREATHLESS WONDER, THE GOD OF THUNDER, MIGHTY THOR 69

4 YOU'VE GOTTA HAVE HEART 109

5 "DOC BRUCE BANNER, BELTED BY GAMMA RAYS, TURNS INTO THE HULK . . ." 133

6 BEYOND THE UNIVERSE 157

APPENDIX: COMPLETE AVENGERS ROSTER 166

ACKNOWLEDGMENTS & IMAGE CREDITS 174

ABOUT THE AUTHOR 175

WHO ARE THE
AVENGERS?

"And there came a day, a day unlike any other, when Earth's mightiest heroes and heroines found themselves united against a common threat. On that day, the Avengers were born—to fight the foes no single super hero could withstand! Through the years, their roster has prospered, changing many times, but their glory has never been denied! Heed the call, then—for now, the Avengers assemble!"

—PROLOGUE FROM *THE AVENGERS*

ACCORDING TO ONE OF THE MOST OFT-TOLD TALES

in the history of comics, the launch of *The Avengers* (cover dated September 1963) can be traced back to a golf game between Martin Goodman, publisher of comics under the Timely and Atlas names, and Jack Liebowitz, publisher of DC Comics in

OPPOSITE: Thor, Hulk, Captain America, and Iron Man.

ABOVE: The book that started it all: *Avengers #1*. Loki was causing problems for the Avengers even back in 1963. Art by Jack Kirby and Dick Ayers.

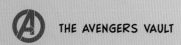

early 1961. Liebowitz was crowing about the sales success of their book, *Justice League of America* (JLA), which gathered DC's colorful crime fighters from a handful of titles and used them as a team.

Goodman had made his fortune spotting and picking up on trends. He was supposedly spurred, as a result of that golf game, to launch a series that would emulate the JLA's success.

Michael Uslan, a movie producer best known for the *Batman* series of films, tells a different story. "I spoke to many people about it, from [former DC Executive Vice President] Irwin Donenfeld to Stan Lee." Donenfeld emphatically told Uslan that neither he nor his father (cofounder of DC) nor Jack Liebowitz could have been involved, if for no other reason than they were not golfers.

According to Uslan: "Martin Goodman was playing with the head of [major distributor] Independent News, Paul Sampliner, an avid golfer. Independent was keeping Goodman's company alive on the heels of the overnight demise of American News in 1957, which distributed Atlas Comics. Sampliner was possibly the single most important man in Goodman's life from 1957 to the early '60s. A competitor playing golf would never reveal sales figures nor tip off Goodman as to what was working best at DC. But a *distributor* who would be profiting from Atlas/Marvel cashing in on a hot new comic-book trend *would* profit and want to see Goodman emulating DC's success. Thus, Sampliner told Goodman about the sales success of *JLA*."

Wherever the impetus came from, Goodman decided to seize on the success of team books. He turned to his cousin, Stanley Lieber—a.k.a. Stan Lee.

Lee and artist Jack Kirby invented a family of heroes and named them the Fantastic Four. After their successful August 1961 debut, Goodman asked for more heroes, sensing the age of heroism was back. In a short period of time, Lee and Kirby were at work on the Incredible Hulk, the Amazing Spider-Man, the Mighty Thor, the Astonishing Ant-Man (and his partner the Wondrous Wasp), and the Invincible Iron Man. By summer 1963, a new age had begun for the company and it rebranded itself from Timely Comics to Marvel Comics.

Lee finally had enough heroes in their own titles to fulfill Goodman's orders, so he introduced *The Avengers*.

He needed a threat sufficient to gather the powerful heroes and apparently decided that nothing less than a god would do: Loki, the Asgardian trickster and enemy of his adopted brother Thor. Loki lured the Hulk into a fresh rampage, prompting the jade-jawed giant's sidekick, teenager Rick Jones, to summon help in the form of a radio call to the Fantastic Four. The radio signal was intercepted by Iron Man, Ant-Man, and Wasp. In short order, Loki's hand was revealed and the heroes ganged up on him.

In the aftermath, it was decided they worked well enough together that they should formally unify, with Wasp picking their team name because it sounded strong.

What was the real-life origin of the team's name? According to Lee, "I really can't recall the thought process. I probably did what I usually do—make up a whole list of probable titles then go down the list and see which both sounds best and looks best when lettered. The Avengers certainly did it for me."

PEOPLE COME AND GO SO QUICKLY HERE

In the second issue, the Avengers took on the Space Phantom. Between issues one and two of the *Avengers*, over in his own series *Tales to Astonish*, Ant-Man learned to grow and became Giant Man. Meanwhile in *Tales of Suspense*, Iron Man was upgrading his armor with regularity.

The Space Phantom imitated various Avengers, sowing dissent. Although the alien was ultimately defeated, his endeavors had long-term consequences. By the issue's end, the Hulk felt—not without cause—that his cohorts didn't trust him and quit the team, immediately upsetting the status quo.

Unlike the JLA's exploits, which were self-contained and could be read in pretty much any order, the *Avengers* series featured ongoing continuity. The following issues dealt with the Hulk, now at war with his former teammates.

THERE SHALL COME A LEADER

The Hulk quickly allied himself with Prince Namor, the Sub-Mariner, a 1940s anti-hero who had made a triumphant return in *Fantastic Four #4*.

In a case of revival cause-and-effect, Namor was directly responsible for the resurrection of his former Golden Age Timely teammate Captain America (having once

ABOVE: Hulk expresses his disgust with his teammates' attitudes and sets into motion an enmity that will last years in Jack Kirby's original art from *Avengers #2*.

retrieved it, and were stunned to see the red, white, and blue costume under the tattered army uniform. A living legend of World War II was reborn!

It wasn't long before Lee realized Cap would become the Avengers' heart and soul.

Lee once wrote, "I had to find a good way to bring back Captain America. I couldn't think of a way to do it. [With] *The Avengers* I had a bunch of other characters for him to play against and react to. Captain America really needs other people to talk to and to be contrasted with, 'cause by himself, he doesn't have quite as colorful a personality as some of our other characters."

Cap took up residence in Avengers Mansion, once owned by Tony Stark and

allied with Cap against threats they could all agree upon, such as Nazis). In *Avengers* #4, while pursuing Namor and the Hulk, the Avengers found a defrosted body,

ABOVE: The Avengers became famous for their cast turnovers, but this was the very first major change to the team. Iron Man, Thor, Giant Man, and the Wasp all departed and were replaced by three former villains: Hawkeye, Quicksilver, and the Scarlet Witch. Art by Jack Kirby and Dick Ayers.

now their high-tech headquarters manned by the unflappable butler, Edwin Jarvis. The finally united team went on to face foes such as the Masters of Evil and the time-traveling Kang the Conqueror.

EARTH'S *MIGHTIEST* HEROES? REALLY?

The title's sixteenth issue featured Captain America on the cover, backed by posters of numerous heroes and villains. By the story's end, the founders had all quit and Cap was left figuring out his next move. As it so happened, three former foes came seeking a second chance. Iron Man held a press conference announcing the roster change and introduced the mutant siblings Quicksilver and the Scarlet Witch, along with archer extraordinaire Hawkeye. The public questioned if these four were really ready to protect the Earth from danger, a question most of the team asked themselves. From the outset, the brash Hawkeye needled Cap, vying for the chairmanship and desperate to prove his worthiness. Fans reacted well, voting Hawkeye their favorite character in 1964.

The company's overall success led Lee to give up the title and turn it over to his new assistant editor, Roy Thomas. The teacher-turned-writer relished a chance to direct the ensemble since he grew up adoring the Justice Society of America, a team of DC's Golden Age heroes that pre-dated the Justice League. He brought back Hawkeye's paramour the Black Widow. The Cold War spy changed allegiances and eventually gained membership. And if the Avengers were once good enough for Thor, the group was obviously good enough for a demigod. Thus Hercules, recently banished from Olympus, arrived and took up residence in the mansion.

But it wasn't all fun and games. Thomas edged the team toward weightier threats such as the Sons of the Serpent, a four-color stand-in for the Ku Klux Klan. The Avengers, after all, were poised to strike, "whenever the deadly poison of bigotry touches us, the flames of freedom burn a little dimmer."

Around this time, artist Don Heck gave way to John Buscema, returning to Marvel after more than a decade of working in the advertising world. The Thomas/Buscema partnership would lead the title into one of its finest periods as it matured into a team greater than the sum of its parts.

turned evil and quickly became one of the Avengers' most persistent, not to mention ever-changing, foes. Ultron in turn crafted his own creation with the intention of having it infiltrate the team. Its name? The Vision.

Ultron's creation was a "synthezoid" (like an android, but . . . uhm . . . synthier). Instead of serving as Ultron's cat's paw, however, the Vision—who yearned for his humanity long before *Star Trek* introduced us to Data—quickly switched sides, becoming a wistful addition to the team. Yet despite the positive development of the Vision's arrival, Hank Pym was still wracked with guilt over having constructed Ultron. This led to Pym's first mental breakdown, prompting him to assume the brash secret identity of Yellowjacket and later stunning the team when he married the Wasp (who, it turned out, knew he was Hank the entire time).

As the Marvel Universe grew in complexity, so did the team's ever-changing roster and the nature of its threats. The book really began to hit its stride in its fifth year of publication, beginning with the arrival of the Black Panther. This period also saw the introduction of Ultron, a Hank Pym–created supercomputer robotic entity that

With Pym now the minuscule Yellowjacket, it wasn't long before Hawkeye decided to power up and use Pym's formula to become the new Goliath.

ABOVE: *Avengers #57* introduced the Vision, an android created by Ultron to attack the Avengers but who joined the team instead. Art by John Buscema and George Klein.

ABOVE: Although he actually showed up in the previous issue, *Avengers #55* featured the first named appearance of the villainous Ultron. Original cover art by John Buscema.

WHO ARE THE AVENGERS?

Colan. Buscema soon returned, only to be followed by his brother Sal, and the adventures continued apace until Thomas decided to kick things up a notch. First came the notion of a parallel universe and a twisted version of the Avengers known as Squadron Sinister. Just over a year later, a different reality introduced Earth's Mightiest Heroes to the Squadron Supreme, a more heroic version of the same characters.

Clearly Thomas felt the time had come to prove that the team was ready

TOTALLY COSMIC

Thomas stayed with the title as artists came and went. Buscema was followed by Gene

to defend the Earth. Picking up loose plot threads and using the cosmology that had been growing since 1961, Thomas plunged

ABOVE: Page 16 of John Buscema's original art from *Avengers #94,* in which the Skrull emperor uses Quicksilver and the Scarlet Witch as bargaining chips to force Captain Marvel to create the formidable Omni-Wave weapon.

THE AVENGERS VAULT

Marvel Earth into the midst of a battle between the Skrulls and their archenemies, the blue-skinned Kree.

What made the cosmic story memorable was not only its scope, but also the photorealistic art by Neal Adams, aided by the brothers Buscema. And Thomas never lost sight of the characters, igniting a subplot that would carry the series for years to come: a romance between the Scarlet Witch and the Vision.

The team survived and endured, reforming and bolstering their ranks in time to handle a threat from Olympus for the title's centennial issue.

Soon after, an overworked Thomas ascended to editor-in-chief as Lee became publisher. With reluctance, Thomas turned the writing over to Steve Englehart, part of the second generation of Marvel creators, who was heavily influenced by Lee and Thomas's works. While Englehart played with the roster and poked around the Marvel Universe, he, like Thomas before him, explored more metaphysical issues.

THE PARTY'S OVER

Englehart's celebrated run kept the title fresh, but it was limited. After a short run

by Gerry Conway, Jim Shooter arrived as the next architect. During this period, a newcomer named George Pérez came to draw the series, honing his skills and displaying a visual flair for groups.

Under Shooter, the roster continued to evolve while also confronting new threats from Ultron and Count Nefaria. Readers really sat up and paid attention, though, when Shooter kicked off the Korvac Saga, as poor everyman Michael Korvac developed unlimited power.

Korvac had been floating around the Marvel Universe since 1975. Originally conceived as a one-shot character by Steve Gerber in *Giant-Size Defenders #3*, he wound up coming back in 1977's *Thor Annual*, written by Roger Stern, who just so happened to be editing *The Avengers* at the time.

Shooter, aided by writer David Michelinie, brought Korvac (who operated in 2997 on a parallel world) to the 20th Century of Earth-616. Later, Earth-616 was established as the world—one in a vast multiverse—in which the "Marvel Universe" is set. By then, Korvac had betrayed humanity to the alien lizardlike Badoon, who rewarded him by making him into a cyborg. When he initially encountered the

Defenders, Korvac was a pawn of the ageless alien called the Grandmaster. Stern's Thor story had Korvac arrive and find Galactus's universe-spanning space station. There he was bathed in the Power Cosmic and gained abilities far beyond those of cybernetic mortals. He first altered his appearance so he could pass as a human and traveled to Earth, intent on turning the world into a utopia of his imagining, forcing the Avengers to intervene.

A team as powerful as the Avengers, Shooter reasoned, needed checks and balances. He created Henry Peter Gyrich, the newly named liaison to the federal government's National Security Council. Gyrich, with his sunglasses and buzz cut (and, some claimed, a passing resemblance to Shooter himself), became an officious thorn in the Avengers' side, especially when he dictated not only the size of the membership, but who the team could welcome

ABOVE: Interior art for *Avengers Finale #1* by Gary Frank and Frank D'Armata.

into its ranks. He insisted the Falcon, an African-American, join the new seven-member configuration to fulfill a racial quota, costing the outraged Hawkeye a post and leading the Falcon to reject membership, not willing to be the team's "token" member.

Shooter also sent Pym down a dark road, disturbing all that had been previously set up. His marriage with Janet Van Dyne, the Wasp, was on the rocks and they bickered. He finally struck her, an act of abuse that horrified Avengers and readers alike. His every act since that moment sought redemption and forgiveness.

AVENGERS COAST-TO-COAST

Hawkeye was still a team player at heart, so he traveled to the opposite coast and

---

ABOVE: *Captain America #117* marks the first appearance of Sam Wilson, a.k.a. the Falcon. Art by Gene Colan and Joe Sinnott.

ABOVE: The cover of *West Coast Avengers #43,* art by John Byrne and Paul Becton, featuring the Scarlet Witch, Hawkeye, Wasp, Tigra, and Wonder Man in action.

founded the West Coast Avengers. The new team attracted an initial roster of Mockingbird (whom Hawkeye would eventually marry), Wonder Man, Tigra, and Iron Man (with Jim Rhodes, not Tony Stark, inside the armor).

This was the first official Avengers spin-off title and it would last nine years (it underwent a name change to Avengers West Coast in 1989).

After Shooter left the helm of the main series, John Byrne wound up writing and drawing both the original book and the West Coast edition, providing tight coordination between the teams.

The spin-off's success led to a tongue-in-cheek story line featuring a team of wannabe heroes calling themselves the Great Lakes Avengers. The misfit team proved popular, notably Squirrel Girl (with command of squirrels, naturally), and they have made recurring appearances ever since.

MEGA ADVENTURES

The writing chores were turned over to Roger Stern, himself a former editor of *The Avengers*. Like Thomas, Stern was steeped in the Marvel mythos and mined it for history that could lead to new revelations.

The roster grew more varied in personality even if the names were the same. A new, female nonalien Captain Marvel joined along with She-Hulk, Tigra, Namor, and the romantic Starfox. Stern also moved the team from the familiar Avengers Mansion to the floating manmade island called Hydrobase, built by Stingray (who briefly joined the roster), although the Hydrobase sunk during a mammoth crossover story line called "Acts of Vengeance."

Since Marvel's heroes successfully banded together in 1984's *Secret Wars*, Marvel would occasionally seek to goose sales, stir up the status quo, and make some noise through various events. With each passing year, the stakes seemed to rise exponentially, sending the heroes through time and space. One such event, the nineteen-part "Operation: Galactic Storm," was inspired by the real world's Operation: Desert Storm, although the opponents in the comics were the martial Kree and the equally combative Shi'ar Empire. Fissures in the deep friendship and trust among the founders began to surface during this story line when Iron Man defied Captain America's orders and executed the Supreme Intelligence. In addition, a Nega-Bomb was

THE *EVOLUTION* OF THE MARVEL UNIVERSE HAPPENS HERE!

detonated, unleashing negative energy in a positive universe—murdering billions of Kree—and letting the Shi'ar annex the surviving worlds, marking the war as Marvel's bloodiest conflict.

The aftermath of this event resonated in story lines for years to come as many of the Kree sought revenge against the Avengers.

But the galactic conflicts paused when Onslaught, a psychic entity, seemingly killed the Avengers and Fantastic Four. It was revealed that Franklin Richards, son of Reed and Sue Richards, used his own nascent psychic powers to fashion a pocket universe where the heroes survived the attack. The "real world" reality was that Marvel actually subcontracted with former Marvel artists Jim Lee and Rob Liefeld, now running their own shops under the Image Comics umbrella, to reboot the flagging series with the brand that would be called "Heroes Reborn." The deal came to an end

ABOVE: *Marvel Onslaught Universe #1 launched the major Onslaught crossover in which Professor X goes crazy and creates the villainous Onslaught. Art by Adam Kubert and Jesse Delperdang.*

 THE AVENGERS VAULT

after a year as the heroes, with much fan-fare, returned to the Marvel Earth-616 in a miniseries entitled "Heroes Return."

"Heroes Return" coincided with new launches of *Fantastic Four, Captain America, Iron Man,* and *The Avengers.* Kurt Busiek was partnered with George Pérez for the third volume of the title, and their run is considered among the best. Busiek had previously written the time-traveling *Avengers Forever* maxi-series and was now working from a clean slate. In addition to the familiar members, the pair augmented their ranks with younger heroes such as Justice, Firestar, Silverclaw, and Triathlon, while pitting the team against many famil-iar foes.

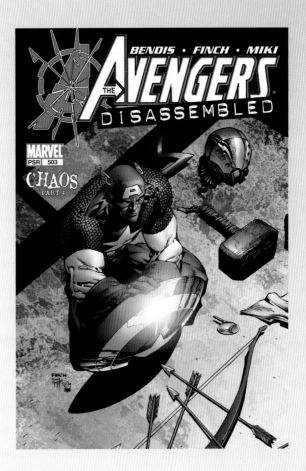

"AVENGERS DISASSEMBLED"

Change was in the wind again. Busiek out-lasted Pérez, but when he left, new writer Brian Michael Bendis brought a different outlook. Bendis had been an indepen-dent creator, writing and drawing his own crime comics before being recruited by Marvel's new editor-in-chief Joe Quesada. Quesada was building a stable of writers that would eventually become the driving force behind Marvel's main story lines and form the creative committee that worked with Marvel Studios.

Bendis knew his continuity but also knew the characters and what made them tick, ensuring they had distinctive voices. The engaging dialogue freshened up the characters and their relationships with one another, even as the world around them crumbled.

A series of relentless, seemingly unre-lated attacks on Earth left the second Ant-Man, Scott Lang, dead and the Avengers Mansion destroyed. The team scrambled

ABOVE: An installment of *Avengers Disassembled #503,* one of the most controversial Avengers stories ever. Art by David Finch and Danny Miki.

to protect the citizenry and figure out what was happening. In time, they realized that the mentally unstable Scarlet Witch, mourning the loss of her magically generated children (introduced years before), was casting spells that warped reality with greater intensity. She had convinced herself that her former teammates were responsible for the children's deaths and threatened everyone until the Sorcerer Supreme, Doctor Strange, used his powerful mystic amulet, the Eye of Agamotto, to calm her. Magneto subsequently arrived to care for his daughter.

But the damage was done. Tony Stark could not fund the repairs, and the devastation to New York City was too great. The team disbanded while a city, in their debt, looked on.

The Scarlet Witch's rehabilitation failed and she used her powers to rid Earth of mutants, robbing millions of their abilities and leaving 198 mutants extant. Events began to build as Quesada, Bendis, and the

ABOVE: *Avengers Disassembled* ran over thirty-seven issues, and began with the Scarlet Witch discovering an awful truth that sent her into madness. Art from issue #503 by Olivier Coipel and Danny Miki.

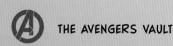

other writers left breadcrumbs and established building blocks. The Marvel Universe was slowly reshaped for a new era.

AVENGERS VS. AVENGERS

One such building block was a revamped Avengers in Bendis's *New Avengers* (drawn by David Finch) as Iron Man, Captain America, Luke Cage, the mutant Wolverine, Ronin (a disguised Echo), Spider-Man, Spider-Woman, and the all-powerful Sentry (no relation to the Kree robots) assembled.

Given all the events swirling around the Marvel United States (and with ready parallels to such real-world developments as the Patriot Act), Congress passed the Super Hero Registration Act, which obligated the heroes to reveal their true identities and be certified to operate by the federal government. While there were positive effects such as training programs to gain newfound powers and abilities, the Act appeared overly intrusive to many heroes. Registration soon became a divisive issue. Captain America saw all the dangers inherent in the law, while Iron Man, now America's Secretary of Defense, had been pushing for the bill for some time. The bill passed after the youthful super hero team, the New Warriors, fought several

villains (including the explosive Nitro) in Stamford, Connecticut; the collateral damage from the battle killed hundreds.

Cap refused orders to apprehend heroes who would not register and wound up leading a resistance movement dubbed the "Secret Avengers" in *New Avengers*, while the newly launched *Mighty Avengers* by Bendis and Frank Cho followed the government-sanctioned team.

ABOVE: By the end of *Avengers Disassembled,* three members were dead. They would return later, but that didn't diminish the initial shock of their demises. Art from #503 by David Finch, Olivier Coipel, and Danny Miki.

WHO ARE THE AVENGERS?

real-world Guantánamo Bay). Cyclops declared mutant neutrality in the matter, although mutant detective team X-Factor broke ranks and came out against the Act.

In the end, it came down to Captain America and Iron Man. Words gave way to fists—until finally Cap, recognizing civilian danger, surrendered. Tony Stark was subsequently named the new director of S.H.I.E.L.D. In the wake of the civil war, it was a fresh beginning—but the enmity among friends took longer to heal.

By this time, it had become apparent that something else was amiss. In short order the Skrulls came out of hiding. They had spent years infiltrating every level of Terran society, replacing human beings with Skrull doppelgangers, all of whom were waiting for the Skrull Queen Veranke to signal the time to act. Elektra, Mockingbird, Hank Pym, and Spider-Woman (Jessica Drew) were exposed as Skrulls, the queen herself replacing Spider-Woman. The *Secret Invasion* nearly

The event sprawled across the entire Marvel Universe as friends fought one another, hero hunted hero, and the villains ran scared as Iron Man and the others rounded them up and locked them away without trial in the extra-dimensional Negative Zone (a veiled allusion to the

ABOVE: *Mighty Avengers #20* was an epilogue to the massive Skrull Invasion story line. Art by Lee Weeks, Jim Cheung, and Jason Keith.

ENCLOSED 1: Ad for *Avengers #3* originally printed in *Avengers #2*. Iron Man's armor would change between the issues. Art by Jack Kirby.

ENCLOSED 2: The 1978 Avengers roster. Art by John Buscema.

the Green Goblin—Spider-Man's deadliest foe—shot and killed her. Now a hero, Osborn literally usurped control of the heroic community, replacing Stark. He disbanded S.H.I.E.L.D. and replaced it with the harsher H.A.M.M.E.R. With government approval, he installed his own version of the Avengers, replacing Hawkeye with the psychopathic Bullseye and Ms. Marvel with Moonstone in the pages of *Dark Avengers*.

During this "Siege," the heroes once more went to ground, thwarting Osborn at every turn until they could expose the madman for the true threat he was.

succeeded until the Wasp seemingly sacrificed her life to stop an attack (she was later revealed to be alive and stuck in the Microverse).

A savage battle broke out, ending when Norman Osborn, also known as

ULTIMATE AVENGERS

In 1999, newly appointed Marvel president Bill Jemas read the Marvel line and decided that nearly forty years of continuity represented an impediment to new readers. He envisioned restarting the Marvel Universe

ABOVE: The cover of the *Ultimates #1*. Art by Brian Hitch and Paul Mounts.

 THE AVENGERS VAULT

from scratch, taking the organic roots and streamlining them for the next generation.

Rather than replace the existing line, he worked with Joe Quesada to launch a new imprint that would reimagine the core heroes and villains for the 21st century. Dubbed the Ultimate line, it launched with *Ultimate Spider-Man* by Brian Michael Bendis and Mark Bagley and proved to be a huge success.

In time, there came a call for a team book, and the Ultimates were born. A government-sponsored operation, it was run by S.H.I.E.L.D. and its director Nicholas Fury. In this world, Fury was redesigned by artist Bryan Hitch as a bald, eye-patched African-American.

General Nick Fury wanted a super-powered strike force to handle a growing number of potent threats. He worked with the scientist couple Henry and Janet Pym and industrialist Tony Stark to form the core of the team, which was to be led by the Super-Soldier Captain America.

"THE HEROIC AGE"

Meanwhile, back on Earth-616, a *Heroic Age* was born after Osborn was incarcerated and the debris of the previous conflicts was tidied up. Former Captain America Steve Rogers (back from the dead) assumed duty as leader of the superpowered community, leaving Bucky Barnes (also back from the dead) to become the new Cap.

The Avengers were reconstituted and newly housed in Stark Tower. The one-time super heroine Jessica Jones, now married to Luke Cage, sometimes aided the team, which now included Iron Fist and the Thing. Rogers asked Victoria Hand, Osborn's former aide de camp, to work as his liaison with the new team.

Change remains a constant with the team and, as 2011 drew to a close, the order changed yet again as another loner, Daredevil, received his membership card.

The team's fortunes have risen and fallen since its debut, but when Earth needed defending or its inhabitants needed help, Earth's Mightiest Heroes could be counted on to act. Their complicated, and at times convoluted, history is rich with acts of heroism and sacrifice—the stuff of modern-day legends.

2

WHEN CAPTAIN AMERICA THROWS HIS MIGHTY SHIELD

FANS WHO WENT TO SEE *CAPTAIN AMERICA: THE First Avenger* in July 2011 witnessed, over previous months, a plethora of films that featured heroes riddled with different degrees of angst. Oftentimes these heroes questioned the very reasons they were doing what they were doing, and even wrestled with the core principles of heroism.

Captain America featured no such indecision. There was no original moral sin committed by the protagonist that drove the rest of his actions. There was no questioning the rightness of his cause or whether he deserved the powers thrust upon him.

OPPOSITE: Captain America, prepared to throw his mighty shield.

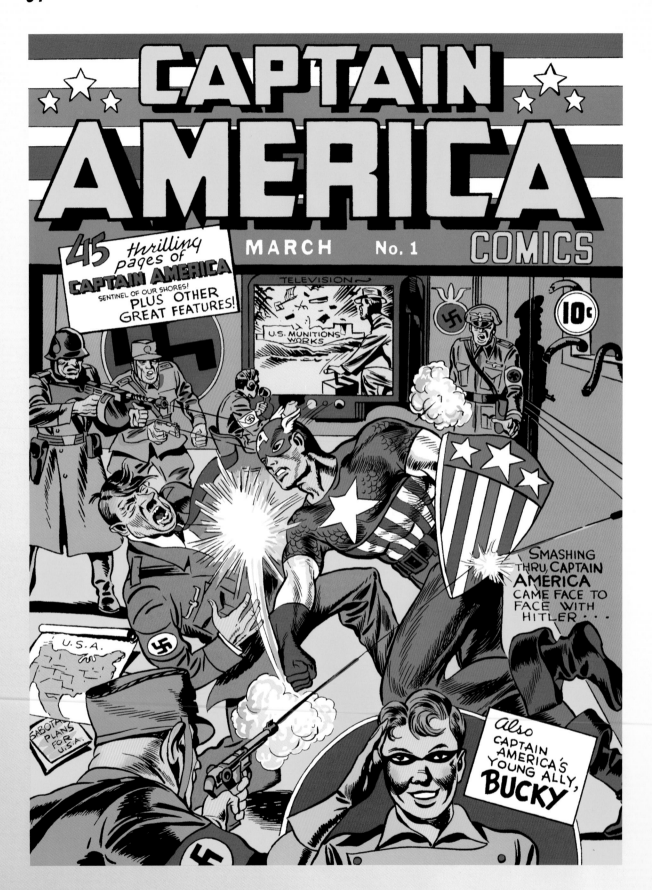

ABOVE: *Captain America #1 was the debut of the patriotic avenger. Art by Jack Kirby, Joe Simon, and Al Liederman.*

What we had instead was Steve Rogers, a scrawny kid in the 1940s, who had the heart of G.I. Joe and the body of Woody Allen. All he cared about was serving his country. When he was given the opportunity, Rogers seized it with both hands and didn't let go.

The confidence is unsurprising—Cap's origin was based in a time perceived as less morally ambiguous. We knew who the bad guys were and where they were. They had uniforms and everything. In fact, it was the bad guys themselves that resulted in Cap's creation.

In his autobiographical *My Life in Comics*, creator Joe Simon wrote:

"The comics that were doing really well at the time were ones with clever villains in them, so I started by looking around for the perfect villain . . . [T]hen I realized that we had the perfect guy right in front of us. I thought to myself, *Let's get a real live villain.* Adolf Hitler would be the perfect foil for our next new character.

"Now we needed a hero who would go up against Hitler . . . We thought it was a good time for a patriotic hero. I did a sketch of him with a chain-mail tunic, and wings on the side of his mask like Mercury, the god from Roman mythology. I gave him a shield, like the ones the knights had carried . . . And that's how Captain America was created!"

OPERATION: REBIRTH

The names have changed, the means have changed, but throughout the years, the basics of Cap's origin have remained consistent: Frustrated 4F would-be soldier Steve Rogers, a New Yorker (of course!), winds up being selected for "Operation: Rebirth." It's a procedure that will create, via a serum and "Vita Rays," the first of a planned army of super-soldiers. Admittedly, there was a bit of irony in the plan—considering that Hitler had more or less the same ambition. But one can excuse the notion of fighting fire with fire. The brains behind the endeavor was Doctor Josef Reinstein (later established to be a code name for Abraham Erskine). Operation: Rebirth proved to be a success, as Steve Rogers became a living incarnation of the old comic ads featuring a scrawny runt getting sand kicked in his face and subsequently transforming himself, through an exercise program, into someone who could beat up any bully.

AND IT *NEEDS* PERFECT BALANCE SO THAT I CAN HANDLE IT LIKE *THIS.!!*

discus version, supposedly because the original bore too strong a resemblance to the chest emblem of the Shield, a character produced by MLJ Magazines. Simon suggested changing the shape of Cap's shield. Problem solved.

Simon pulled from the origin of another hero that he'd created: Blue Bolt, published by Novelty Press. Blue Bolt, a.k.a. Fred Parrish, acquired his powers through an injection courtesy of a scientist named Bertoff.

The Super Serum remained a component of the origin. It was retconned (what modern fans call a retroactive continuity implant that changes history but pretends that it was, in fact, always that way) in *Tales of Suspense #63* as having been taken orally. *Captain America #109* later established that Steve was subjected to the mythical Vita-Rays, a catalyst required to activate

But the arrival of a Nazi spy (later named Heinz Kruger) prevented the program from reaching its full potential. Kruger gunned down Reinstein/Erskine, who unfortunately had committed key sections of the formula to memory, thus making it impossible to replicate. The government transformed Steve Rogers into a symbol of its battle against the forces of the Axis powers, and thus Captain America was born.

The shield that Joe Simon's partner, Jack Kirby, designed for him lasted all of one issue. It was replaced by the better-known

ABOVE: Art from *Tales of Suspense #62*, by Jack Kirby and Vince Colletta.

the Serum and enable it to achieve full potency. The one-of-a-kind Vita-Ray machine was destroyed and again—of course—Erskine left no plans behind that would enable it to be recreated. In the limited series *The Adventures of Captain America* we also learned that pretransformation Cap received rigorous physical training so that not all of his strength was courtesy of medical science.

Perhaps it's appropriate that the symbol of America had to change to keep up with evolving American mores.

THE WAR EFFORT

For reasons that were never made especially clear, other than that secret identities were de rigueur at the time, Steve Rogers was assigned to Camp Lehigh in Virginia under the terribly clever cover name of "Steve Rogers," a bumbling infantry private who had the habit of disappearing every time Captain America showed up. He also

had a personal firearm, but his shield eventually proved to be such a capable offensive weapon, with his ability to fling it like a Frisbee from hell, that he gave up the gun.

Keeping in line with the same philosophy that required super heroes to have

---

ABOVE: In *Captain America #109,* Cap relates his origin to an attentive Nick Fury. Art by Jack Kirby and Syd Shores.

WHEN CAPTAIN AMERICA THROWS HIS MIGHTY SHIELD

ABOVE: A sequence from *Captain America #1*. Art by Jack Kirby, Joe Simon, and Al Liederman.

double identities, Cap also acquired a sidekick.

His name was James Buchanan "Bucky" Barnes. The young teen was the camp mascot (eventually explained as being made a ward of the state after the death of his father in basic training). Bucky accidentally walked in on Steve while he was changing into (or out of) his Cap uniform. Bucky promptly said he would keep Steve's secret, but only if Steve trained him to be his sidekick. Steve readily agreed to Bucky's terms.

Still, since the United States hadn't officially entered the war yet, and Nazis weren't exactly overrunning Virginia, Cap had to find other diversions for his time. According to Joe Simon, "[I]t really was a horror mystery book . . . [M]ost of the stories were adventures like 'Case of the Black Witch' and 'The Hunchback of Hollywood and the Movie Murder.' Sure, we had stories such as 'Trapped in the Nazi Stronghold,' but most of them weren't like that."

Cap's debut was an immediate hit, selling nearly a million copies. After the United States entered World War II, the gloves would come off in terms of taking on the Nazis. Eventually Cap even found common cause with such acerbic characters as the Sub-Mariner. Cap and Bucky would team up with him, along with the Human Torch, the unfortunately named "Whizzer," and other characters to form the All-Winners Squad. It was a short-lived team to be sure—lasting two issues—but they laid the framework for the 1970s *Invaders,* a longer-lived series of adventures depicting Cap, Subby, and Torch banding together to battle the Nazi menace.

In the real world, after World War II, Captain America—who had been featured not only in his own book but also in such titles as *Marvel Mystery Comics, USA Comics,* and *All Star Comics*—faded from sight. He was briefly revived, along with other Marvel heroes, in the 1950s, battling against the new bugaboo of the time: Communists. But Captain America, Commie Smasher, didn't play nearly as well as Captain America, scourge of the Nazis. It was understandable: Cap was, after all, created specifically to be an opponent for Adolf Hitler. Communism fears were, more often than not, paranoia unleashed. Cap was better suited for the black-and-white, pure evil of Hitler and his Nazis.

In the world of comic-book continuity, however, Cap's eventual disappearance

the nefarious Baron Zemo.

A MAN OUT OF TIME

In the coincidences upon which Silver-Age comics typically thrived, Captain America was discovered frozen in a block of ice by the Sub-Mariner, who was up in the North Sea. At the time, Cap—in suspended animation—was being worshipped by Inuit. Namor happened to be in a bad mood, probably because it was a day ending in the letter "y," and so the irked sea king—not realizing his former teammate was inside the block—chucked him into the

had nothing to do with the changing tastes of readers or problems in the publishing industry. Instead it was deeply rooted in the activities of the original villains that Cap was created to combat: particularly

water. Eventually the ice floated into the warmer climes of the Gulf Stream. The warmer waters caused Cap to thaw out and presumably, left to his own devices, he would have drowned had the Avengers

ABOVE: In an iconic moment, the Avengers come upon the unconscious, newly thawed body of Captain America in *Avengers #4.* Art by Jack Kirby, George Roussos, and Stan Goldberg.

not cruised by and plucked him from death's grasp.

Once he came around, Cap greeted the Avengers in the time-honored method that super heroes typically employ upon first encountering each other: he tried to fight them. After he calmed down, Captain America explained to them how he had come to this unlikely pass, and the fate of his partner, Bucky.

He described how the dynamic pair had endeavored to halt an experimental drone plane, armed with an explosive device. In the original recounting, the architect of the scheme was hidden in shadow; only in the next issue would he be revealed as the nefarious Baron Zemo.

Cap and Bucky were on a motorcycle, pursuing the rocket.

Bucky made it to the rocket, but Cap fell short. The rocket then exploded,

ABOVE: Captain America snaps out of his decades-long slumber and is fighting within one panel of waking up. Art by Jack Kirby, George Roussos, and Stan Goldberg.

ABOVE: Rick Jones, aspiring to take over as Cap's sidekick, tries on Bucky's uniform in *Captain America #110*. Art by Jim Steranko and Joe Sinnott.

presumably killing Bucky Barnes and sending Cap plummeting into the waters of the North Atlantic.

However unlikely the circumstances that had brought Captain America to his new situation, there was no denying the result: the Avengers had inadvertently stumbled upon the guy who was born to be their leader.

Still, Captain America had left behind him the Golden Age of super heroes, where personalities were simple and mission statements were clear. Instead he had been deposited into the burgeoning Marvel Age, where the heroes were—for the most part—a morass of frustrations, guilty feelings, and emotional entanglements. Cap's state of mind fit right in. He spent many issues having issues, mostly boiling down to two things: He felt out of place since the world had changed so much between the 1940s and the 1960s, and he felt guilty for the death of Bucky. So much so that he tried to replace him with Bucky lookalike Rick Jones . . . a rare lapse in strategic planning from the Super Soldier since anyone could tell you that trying to bogart the Hulk's sidekick is a bad move.

In retrospect, he should have considered himself lucky. The Cap of the films goes missing in the 1940s only to wake up in the twenty-first-century world of cell phones, the Internet, and reality television. As for Bucky, well . . . not dead, as it turned out. But that would come later.

THE MANY FACES OF CAPTAIN AMERICA

Things change. It's both the Marvel way (different Thors, different Iron Men, different Spider-Men) and the American way. So when you've got a Marvel hero named Captain America, change isn't just inevitable—it's practically a moral imperative. Captain America has gone through a variety of incarnations, both in terms of the people in the Captain America costume and also the identities assumed by Steve Rogers himself.

CAPTAIN AMERICA: 1945–1950S

Sure, *Avengers #4* asserted that Steve Rogers vanished in 1945. Yet, like a guest at a party who's stayed too long, Cap appeared to be hanging around for another fifteen years. Turns out they were all different guys.

William Nasland operated out of Philadelphia as the costumed adventurer "Spirit of '76," presumably inspired

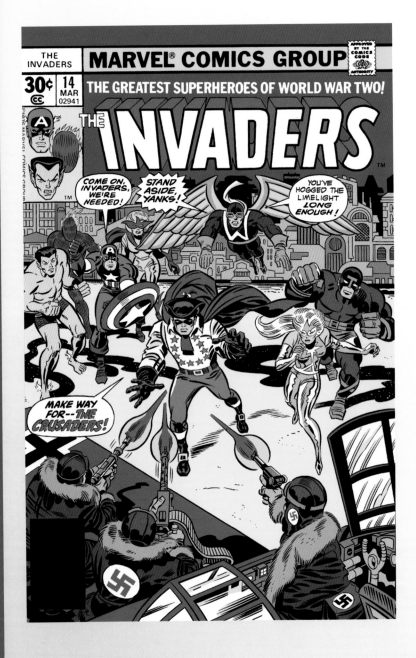

no one's hearts). Nasland died in action during an adventure with the All-Winners Squad, battling a fiendish plot to replace then-congressional candidate John F. Kennedy with a robot. The dying Nasland was found by . . .

Jeffrey Mace. Mace was a reporter and correspondent for the New York *Daily Bugle*, the newspaper that—decades later—would harass Spider-Man. Mace, like Nasland, was inspired to create his own patriotic hero identity, appropriately named the Patriot. He even fought alongside Cap and Bucky as part of a separate group called the Liberty Legion. Upon Cap's demise, the Patriot took up the mantle of Captain America (not really that much of a stretch when you think about it) and kept Bucky on as his sidekick. Eventually Mace retired from crime fighting in 1950, following the lead of Bucky/ Fred who had retired the previous year after being wounded in action. This cleared the decks for . . .

William Burnside. Arguably Captain America's biggest fan, Burnside—who

by Cap's example. After Cap and Bucky's disappearance, Nasland was personally recruited by President Harry S. Truman to take Cap's place, with a young man named **Fred Davis** selected to impersonate Bucky (since presumably the team of "Captain America and Fred" would strike fear into

---

ABOVE: *Invaders #14* features the short-lived Crusaders, whose members included the Spirit of '76, a.k.a. William Nasland. He would later be the first man to replace Captain America. Art by Jack Kirby.

ABOVE: A page from *Captain America Annual #6,* art by Ron Wilson, which features Jeffrey Mace. He began his career as the Patriot in 1941 and was the third man to become Captain America.

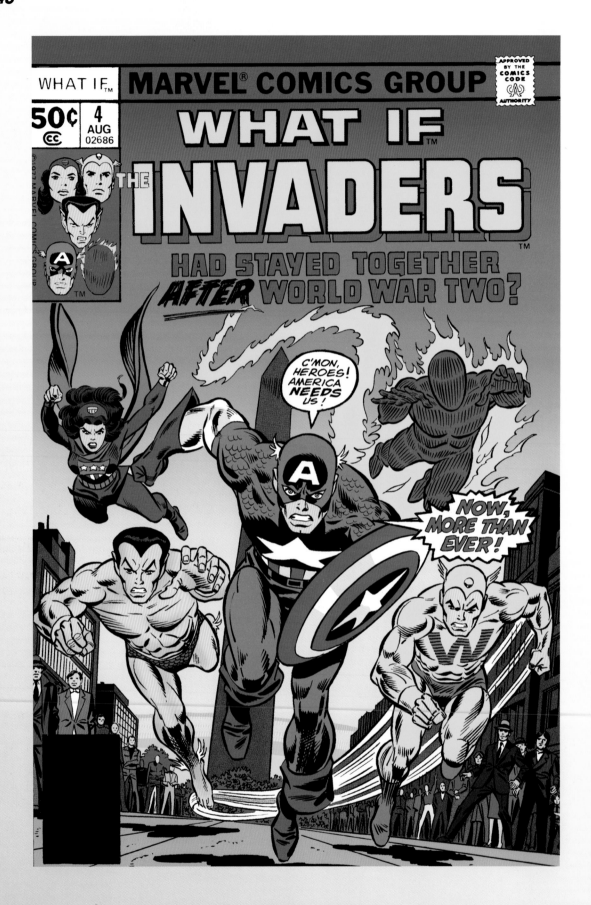

ABOVE: *What If?* #4 is the definitive story of the death of William Nasland, passing the Captain America mantle to Jeffrey Mace. Art by Gil Kane and Frank Giacola.

graduated with a PhD in American history and did his thesis on Cap—came across the plans for the original Super-Soldier formula while examining old Nazi files in 1953. Burnside brought his findings to the FBI and volunteered to become the fourth man to bear the name "Captain America," because the fighting men in Korea needed a symbol, too. He even went so far as to legally change his name to "Steve Rogers."

This endeavor required that Burnside/ Rogers completely reconstruct his face via plastic surgery and alter his voice so that he would be a dead ringer for the real Steve Rogers. Why would this be necessary since he'd be wearing a mask and two previous Captain Americas hadn't worried about imitating his voice? No clue. Anyway, the procedure took so long that by the time it was finished, so was the Korean War. So the FBI set up Burnside/Rogers as a teacher at a Connecticut prep school called Lee. (Lee High. Lehigh. Get it?) There Burnside/Rogers began sporting glasses and struck up a friendship with a young student, **Jack Monroe.**

Eventually they took up costumed adventuring together. If that sounds kind of insane, well, in this case it quite literally was. In order to carry off their identities, "Rogers" and Monroe injected themselves with the Super-Soldier formula. But without the Vita-Rays to stabilize the process, their minds started to deteriorate and they began to see Communists everywhere. The FBI finally captured them and put them into suspended animation.

All, or at least most, of this was revealed in *Captain America* issues 153–156. The story was scripted by Steve Englehart, but according to Roy Thomas:

"It was my basic notion. I was determined to cover the period between 1945 (when Stan had had Cap frozen, *Avengers #4*) and the recent past, say 1964. So, when Steve Englehart became the writer, I, shall we say, suggested that he account for the 1950s Cap. I believe I meant for him to handle the late '40s as well, but he didn't—although he did a fine job in *Captain America*—because, after all, we had reprinted a story or two from that period (the two *All-Winners Squad* stories) as well as many of the 1950s Cap stories. Thus, in 1976, I wrote the always-canonical *What If #4* with Frank Robbins, accounting for the 1945–49 Cap. Actually I made him *two* people: the Spirit of '76, introduced in *The Invaders*, who got killed in Cap uniform in *What If #4*, and the Patriot, who took over at the end of that issue. Never did account for why that Cap 'retired' circa 1949, leaving a new Cold War–era Cap to come into being in 1953, the date of *Young Men #24*. That's my idea of a good time."

NOMAD

In early 1974, Steve Rogers had reached a crisis point in his career. A battle with the underground organization called the Secret Empire had revealed corruption in the government that, it was implied, led directly to then-president Richard M. Nixon. This revelation of corruption destroyed Steve's faith in the government and made him feel that Captain America symbolized something that no longer existed. For a time Rogers was content to fight the good fight as a member of the New York City Police Department. But after a confrontation in *Captain America #179* with a villain called the Golden Archer (who turned out to be a disguised Hawkeye endeavoring to lure Steve back into super heroing), Steve decided to return to costumed action . . . if for no

other reason, presumably, than to prevent any more of his friends from doing something similarly idiotic to bring him back.

But his feeling that the ideals Captain America represented were out of date hadn't changed, so he created a new identity: the Nomad.

Nomad's debut was less than stellar. Squaring off against the Serpent Squad, he was close to defeating them when he tripped over his cape, allowing the villains to get away.

Nomad's cape was gone in short order. Nomad himself didn't last much longer after a short-lived substitute for Captain America—**Roscoe Simons**, a mechanic by trade and devoted Cap fan—was brutally murdered by the Red Skull in *Captain America #183*. Upon learning of Roscoe's death, Steve declared, "There has to be somebody who'll fight for the dream, against any foe . . . Somebody who'll do the job I started—Right! And God knows I can't let anyone else run the risks that job entails for me!" The epiphany came too late to save Roscoe, but at least Steve Rogers was back behind the mask.

Comics being comics, however, nothing is allowed to go to waste. Remember

ABOVE: The cover of *Captain America #179,* in which Cap battles the Golden Archer, later revealed to be Hawkeye in disguise. Art by Ron Wilson and Frank Giacola.

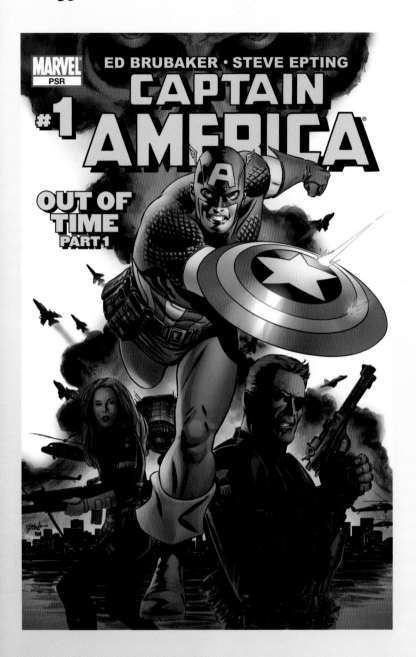

and killed by a cyborg assassin who was revealed to be the Winter Soldier.

Who was the Winter Soldier? Yeah . . . you're gonna love this . . .

BUCKY BARNES

Remember Bucky? Remember how it was revealed that he died?

Even in 1945, they just weren't building exploding drone planes the way they used to.

In *Captain America vol. 5, #1*, the Red Skull—one of Captain America's most frequent opponents—had managed to cobble together his very own Cosmic Cube, a long-standing Marvel device of incredible power (as anything with the name "cosmic" in it tends to be). He dismissed out of hand the efforts of a KGB agent named Lukin to acquire it, only to be promptly blown away by an assassin. This was the first appearance of Winter Soldier, the shooter. Meanwhile, Steve Rogers informed his former lover, Sharon Carter, that he had been having recurring dreams about his wartime adventures with Bucky. Steve was

Jack Monroe? The psychotic Bucky from the 1950s? Eventually he was rehabilitated, took up Rogers's "Nomad" identity, and became Cap's partner for a time before striking out on his own. Later, unfortunately, Monroe began to have relapses and psychotic breaks, and was eventually shot

ABOVE: The Winter Soldier, a formidable opponent, first appears in *Captain America Vol. 5, #1*. Art by Steve Epting.

somewhat prescient, as the Winter Soldier was revealed to be a brainwashed Bucky.

Turned out that the Soviets managed to beat the Avengers to

prevented him from bleeding out). Brain damage gave him amnesia, the Russians gave him a cybernetic arm, and the Winter Soldier was off

the punch by nearly two decades in the use-a-sub-to-find-the-frozen-body-of-a-patriotic-American-hero game. They found a post-explosion Bucky floating in the frigid waters, minus an arm (presumably the icy water

to the races. When the Soviets weren't using him for assassinations and other wet work, they kept him in a cryogenic stasis. Consequently he aged only minimally during the intervening decades.

ABOVE: In *Captain America Vol. 5, #11,* the Winter Soldier is revealed to be none other than Bucky Barnes. Art by Steve Epting and Mike Perkins.

done, Bucky fled the scene.

He later returned as Winter Soldier, fighting on the side of the good guys this time, but after the shooting (and supposed death) of Steve Rogers, Bucky—at Tony Stark's suggestion—became the new Captain America.

Bucky reigned as the new Captain America for a time, and eventually learned that Steve Rogers was, in fact, not dead at all. Yet at the end of the one-shot book entitled *Captain America: Who Will Wield the Shield?*, Steve Rogers turned his shield over to Bucky and told him to continue the good fight permanently as the red, white, and blue Avenger.

The whole origin was revealed some issues later and, with Steve Rogers's help, Bucky managed to remember who he was and recapture his true identity. Horrified by the recollections of the terrible things he'd

Apparently Steve had forgotten his own speech back in *Captain America #183*. He'd be reminded in the third issue of *Fear Itself,* a company-wide crossover in which poor Bucky was—once again—thought to be killed.

ABOVE: *All-New Captain America #1. Art by Stuart Immonen.*

It's not all that shocking. When he's not holding his shield on his arm, Cap tends to sling it around his shoulders. So what else can you expect but a high mortality rate for someone who literally has a target on his back?

A NEW CAPTAIN, A NEW ERA

In July 2014, Marvel announced that Steve Rogers will pass the mantle of Captain America to Sam Wilson, a.k.a. the Falcon. While this isn't the first time the Falcon has donned the star spangled suit (he filled in when Cap was presumed dead in *Captain America: Sentinel of Liberty #8–9*), Sam comes from a different generation and doesn't have a military background—he's a modern man guided by his own morality. That, and the fact that the embodiment of America is now black, clearly signals a new era. Rick Remender and Stuart Immonen begin this new chapter in *All-New Captain America #1*.

BAD GUYS

First came the villain: Adolf Hitler. Captain America was created to take him down a peg. In that respect, he succeeded,

probably better than his creators could have expected. According to Joe Simon, the Nazi Bund—an American Nazi group established in the 1930s—"didn't like the cover of the first issue, which made light of their beloved Fuhrer and his hordes . . . They were constantly threatening us, to the point that we had police stationed outside of our offices, and the FBI got involved. That didn't

---

ABOVE: Sam Wilson's previous appearance as Captain America in *Sentinel of Liberty #9*. Art by Dougie Braithwaite, Dan Green, and John Costanza.

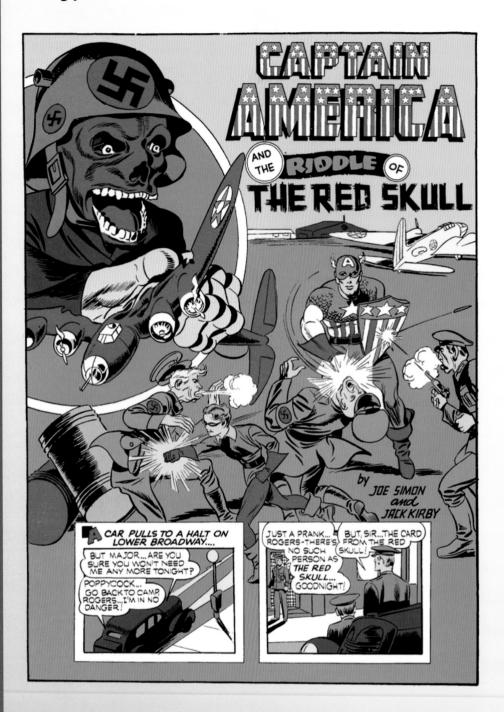

him a hard time over the years. Many have their roots in World War II, proving that villains are—if nothing else—sore losers who carry a grudge. Here's a sampling of the more notable ones.

THE RED SKULL

Cap's premiere villain began his life as something truly evil: a dessert topping.

Seriously. Joe Simon was sitting in a Times Square restaurant with a hot fudge sundae in front of him, trying to come up with a major opponent for his newly created hero. Contemplating the confection before him, the hot fudge dribbling down the side "looked like limbs—legs, feet, and hands—and I'm thinking to myself, *Gee, this'd make an interesting*

stop the Bund members from following us around and taunting us."

Clearly Cap had the last laugh in that regard. But his triumph hasn't deterred an impressive array of villains from giving

---

ABOVE: *Captain America #1* splash page for the debut of the Red Skull. Art by Jack Kirby and Joe Simon.

villain . . . *We'll call him Hot Fudge . . . Just put a face on him, and have him ooze all over the place.*"

After doing some preliminary sketches that looked as absurd as you can probably imagine, Simon dismissed the idea as being unbelievable. "But I looked again at the sundae, and I saw the big cherry on top. The cherry looked like a skull. 'Wow,' I said to myself. 'Red Skull . . . *that* sounds good. And it made a lot more sense.'"

Simon went on to say that the Red Skull "was only supposed to appear once. We killed him off in the very first story, and I never thought anybody would remember him. But they did—they clamored for us to bring him back."

And bring him back they did. Repeatedly.

There have literally been too many iterations of the Red Skull to cover in this space. So we will confine ourselves to the first and best known: German-born Johann Schmidt, whose mother died in childbirth and whose father committed suicide the following day. After running away from an orphanage, he held a series of jobs until he eventually worked as a bellhop in a hotel where—as fate would have it—Adolf Hitler

ABOVE: *Captain America #16* features the return of the Red Skull. Art by Al Avison.

wound up staying. Berating one of his officers, Hitler pointed at Schmidt and swore that he could train a bellboy to do a better job than his underling. Upon scrutinizing Schmidt, he declared, "The way you look at me! The envy, the jealousy in your eyes! The sheer blazing hatred! I know these emotions! You too hate all mankind! What an inspiration this gives me! You shall be my greatest achievement! I shall make a perfect Nazi of you! You will serve me! You will be my right arm! You will never fail me!"

Hitler provided Schmidt with extensive training and, ultimately, a snappy red mask. From that point on Captain America, in pretty much all his incarnations, would battle the Red Skull, his imposters, and his increasingly grandiose plans to conquer everything in sight.

BARON ZEMO

The moniker describes one of—or more accurately, two of—the best-known Captain America villain(s), right after the Red Skull.

The first of the Barons was Heinrich Zemo, the mastermind behind the plot that supposedly killed Bucky and sent Captain America into deep freeze for two decades. He was never actually present during the original run of Captain America stories back in the 1940s, although he did show up in an issue of *Sergeant Fury and His Howling Commandos* in the 1960s, effectively inserting him into Cap's history retroactively. Indeed, the good sergeant was as key a player in Zemo's history as Cap: when Fury and the Howlers invaded Zemo's castle and destroyed his death ray, the abashed Zemo fled with his family and took to wearing what would become his trademark purple cowl in order to cover his shame.

His choice of headgear would become a permanent fashion statement when, while brewing up a solution called Adhesive X (possibly to glue together mutants) Zemo was interrupted by the unexpected arrival of Captain America. One slung shield and a broken container later, the adhesive spilled all over Zemo's head, permanently affixing his cowl to his head and face. This provided him with a deep-seated grudge against Captain America. In later years he would clash with Captain America and the Avengers.

After a series of plans that were thwarted by Cap and the Avengers, Baron Zemo—in a move worthy of *Phineas and Ferb*'s incompetent Doctor Doofenshmirtz—wound up

ABOVE: Original art by Jack Kirby of page 4 from *Avengers #6* shows the battle between Captain America and Baron Zemo. The fight results in Zemo's mask glued to his face.

WHEN CAPTAIN AMERICA THROWS HIS MIGHTY SHIELD

resulted in bringing down an avalanche on himself.

The disaster cleared the way for the good Baron's son, Helmut Zemo. Utterly devoted to his father, Helmut blamed Captain America for his father's death and subsequently took on both Cap and the Cap's then-partner, the Falcon. Helmut managed to outdo his father, not in the evil-accomplishment category, but in the screwing-himself-up category as he wound up falling into an entire vat of Adhesive X. The accident gave him hideous facial scars and even greater enmity toward Captain America, if such was possible. He was eventually killed but,

suffering the ultimate super villain indignity of causing his own demise when his attempt to fire his aptly named death ray

ABOVE: *Captain America #168* includes the debut of Baron Zemo's son who will go on to be the new Baron Zemo. Art by John Tartag, George Roussos, and Linda Lessmann.

unlike his father, he managed to return repeatedly to assail Cap through a variety of means.

ARNIM ZOLA

Arnim Zola—who first showed up in *Captain America #208*—was a Swiss scientist during World War II who was quite possibly the first researcher into genetic engineering. He brought his findings to Adolf Hitler with the notion of creating a clone of der Fuhrer should anything go wrong—a concept that Hitler readily embraced. An ally of the Red Skull, Zola kept a low profile, working out of a castle in South America that was—as most Nazi castles tended to be—destroyed by American comic-book heroes.

Dwarfish by birth, Zola created a genetically engineered body for himself that was certain not to draw unwanted attention, with an ESP box instead of a head and a three-dimensional image of his face

ABOVE: Captain America faces off against Arnim Zola in *Captain America #209*. Art by Jack Kirby, Frank Giacola, and George Roussos.

WHEN CAPTAIN AMERICA THROWS HIS MIGHTY SHIELD

ABOVE: Captain America first meets the venomous MODOK in *Tales of Suspense #94*. Art by Jack Kirby and Joe Sinnott.

on his chest. The ESP box could generate energy blasts of 100,000 volts, and the body itself made Zola effectively immortal, enabling him to spend an eternity getting his butt kicked by Captain America.

MODOK

George Tarleton was a scientist working for a nefarious outfit called AIM (Advance Idea Mechanics), an organization of evil scientists specializing in seeking power. Tarleton was selected to be a human guinea pig to test the power limits of the Cosmic Cube, and as a result, Tarleton mutated into a huge-headed grotesquerie in a floating chair, with superhuman intelligence and psionic powers. He was dubbed MODOC (Mobile Organism Designed Only for Computing) but promptly destroyed his creators and redubbed himself MODOK (Mobile Organism Designed

Only for Killing), probably because this was a more terrifying name than MOOK (Mobile Organism for Only Killing).

MODOK first showed up in *Tales of Suspense #93*, the split-book that Cap shared with Iron Man until the armored hero eventually received his own title a couple years later. Since then MODOK has shown up to harass Cap (and also the Hulk) numerous times, initially as the leader of AIM until he was deposed. Eventually he was annihilated,

ABOVE: Interior art from *Tales of Suspense #94,* by Jack Kirby and Joe Sinnott.

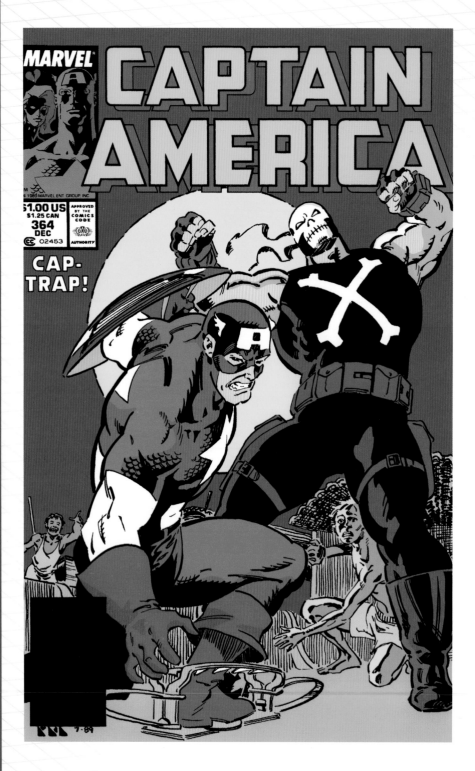

CROSSBONES

Crossbones, born Brock Rumlow, was a Neo-Nazi who made his first appearance in *Captain America #359* in shadow (since many of Cap's villains tended to be shy when they first showed up). A gang leader in his youth, he wound up in a school for criminals run by the villainous Taskmaster. He excelled so thoroughly in hand-to-hand combat and marksmanship that within a few years he became a teacher there.

Eventually, as was practically a requirement for Cap's opponents, he teamed up with the Red Skull, although he was more of an underling than a partner. It was the Skull

but AIM was apparently not smart enough to learn from previous mistakes and revived him using the Cosmic Cube.

who dubbed him "Crossbones," which was a far better evil alias than his other nickname, "Bingo" (no, we're not kidding).

ABOVE: Cap slugs it out with Crossbones in *Captain America #364*. Art by Kieron Dwyer.

ENCLOSED 1: An authentic Sentinels of Liberty fan club membership card from 1941.

ENCLOSED 2: John Romita's original cover art and color guide for *Captain America #114*.

ABOVE: *Tales of Suspense #75* marks the first appearance of Batroc the Leaper. Art by Jack Kirby, Dick Ayers, and John Tartaglione.

Crossbones worked his way through the Marvel Universe, attempting (and failing) to assassinate such luminaries as the Kingpin and Gambit. Eventually he was implicated in the "death" of Captain America, captured, and beaten up by Wolverine while in S.H.I.E.L.D. custody.

BATROC THE LEAPER

George Batroc—or, as he might call himself, Batroc Zee Leaper—first sprung to attention in *Tales of Suspense* #75 and was as close to comic relief as a Cap villain ever got. A criminal mercenary and master of the French martial art of *savate* (i.e. kick fighting), Batroc was unintentionally hilarious. He spoke with a ludicrously thick French accent that would remind any modern reader of the taunter from *Monty Python and the Holy Grail*.

In the old days, Cap's biggest challenge when Batroc showed up was keeping a straight face while pummeling him. In more recent times, however, Batroc has occasionally been treated with more respect by writers, depicted as far more formidable and played less for humorous effect (although his daughter kept up the family tradition of being ineffectual by getting outmatched

by Taskmaster). Batroc has split his time between working with teams, operating as an independent mercenary, and surrendering.

THE FIRST AMONG AVENGERS

What is it about Captain America? Although he was a latecomer to the team (by only a few issues, but still . . .), Cap was quickly accepted as first among equals. In the presence of a scientific genius, a millionaire industrialist, and a god, somehow this simple guy from New York—with no powers other than his athleticism, cunning, and shield—became the de facto leader of the group. Why is that?

When asked about it, Stan Lee settled on a fairly practical answer: "I'd guess it's because he's the only one with military combat experience. Also, how does a guy named 'Captain America' *not* become the leader?"

Roy Thomas opined, "I'm not real big on theories about that type of thing, but it's clear that somehow—probably something about the costume, since we never knew much about Steve Rogers in the '40s otherwise—he was the guy everyone looked to to lead. In the *All-Winners Squad*'s two issues, he was their leader if they had one, despite being the only one without superpowers

took a hike at the same time."

Ultimately one supposes that there's simply a timelessness about him, even if he did wind up a man out of his natural time period. And that timelessness, combined with his endless ability to strategize and outwit his opponents, makes Cap the go-to guy when you want to win a battle.

As it turned out, he wouldn't be the only member of the Avengers who'd had the world around him change dramatically. You think Cap had it

[not counting Bucky—and that's assuming you don't count becoming a supreme physical specimen from an injection a superpower]. Although he became the leader in the Avengers almost by default when Thor, Iron Man, and Giant-Man all

tough adjusting to the differences between the modern world and the 1940s? Imagine when you've been around for centuries, like our next Avenger.

ABOVE: Cover art for *All-Winners #1*. Art by Alex Schomburg.

ABOVE: A timeless hero shown on the cover of *Captain America: Living Legend #1*. Art by Adi Granov.

3

BEHOLD IN BREATHLESS WONDER, THE GOD OF THUNDER, MIGHTY THOR

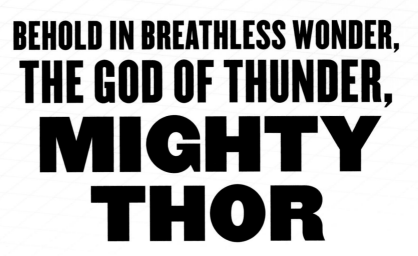

IN ANCIENT TIMES, GODS STEMMED FROM LEGENDS created by humans to explain what they did not understand. Ancient people looked to the skies and saw lightning and the pure unbridled power of a thunderstorm, and they attributed it to great, unseen beings. The Greeks would speak of Zeus, the thunderer; the Romans would call him Jupiter. Over the centuries the Old English name of Thunor came into use and eventually the Vikings started referring to the thunder god by the name for which he's best known: Thor ("Thorr" in the old spelling).

OPPOSITE: The Mighty Thor swings his hammer.

Thor went forth against Jörmungand.

goats, which—if Thor was hungry, as he often was—could be devoured and then brought back to life through the simple means of laying their bones upon their skins. His most formidable weapon was a battle hammer called Mjolnir (pronounced *mee-YOLE-neer*). Mjolnir means "crusher" and, according to the Prose Edda—a collection of poems detailing many Norse legends—was crafted for Thor by the dwarf Sindri.

Thor is described as having fiery red hair and a matching beard, and he sported a magic belt and a pair of iron gloves that

Thor (for whom Thursday, Thor's Day, was named) was the son of Odin or Woden (for whom Wednesday was named) and Frigga or Freya (for whom Friday was named). He was married to the goddess Sif, had an assortment of offspring, and rode around in a chariot pulled by enabled him to lift Mjolnir. Along with the other Norse deities, he resided in Asgard, the home of the gods that was connected to Earth (Midgard) via a rainbow bridge called Bifrost. He had the kind of excitable, unpredictable temperament that one would expect from a god closely associated

---

ABOVE: Thor's exploits have been told for centuries and are seen here in an illustration from *The Heroes of Asgard: Tales from Scandinavian Mythology.*

with nature, considering nature's random and occasionally destructive nature. When Vikings heard thunder and saw lightning flashing, it meant he was battling frost giants or similar foes. One time he was engaged in a drinking contest and attempted to drink the sea dry. He failed in the endeavor, but he did manage to lower the sea level and was thus responsible for the first tide. This was the same god who once consumed an entire ox, eight salmon, and three barrels of mead in one sitting; his appetites were, to put it mildly, prodigious.

Then again, if one knows their own doom, one might tend to live for the moment.

Most, if not all, mythologies have some manner of creation myth. The Vikings had a detailed and specific end-of-days scenario. The twilight of the gods, typically referred to as Ragnarok, outlined exactly how the gods would die. Thor's father, Odin, was destined to be devoured by the monstrous Fenris wolf, while Thor would square off against Jormungand, a.k.a. the Midgard Serpent—the monstrous beast that spans the entirety of the globe. Thor would actually manage to dispatch Jormungand, but he would then take

ABOVE: An illustration of Thor by Jack Kirby from *The Mighty Thor #131*.

nine paces and drop dead from the serpent's poison.

A WARRIOR BORN

The narrative of the Marvel Comics incarnation of the thunder god was hardly linear. His "origin," as presented in *Journey into Mystery #83*, turned out to be the result of machinations that stretched back centuries.

His creative origins stemmed from discussions between Stan Lee and Jack Kirby about their next super hero creation. According to Lee:

"Jack said, 'We've got the Hulk who's so strong, and Spider-Man who can climb walls. What can we do now?' And it occurred to me that the only thing we could do, perhaps, was come up with a god. I thought it would be fun to make a god a hero."

It certainly made creative sense, especially when considering Marvel's competition. Superman was, to all intents and purposes, a god. A hero who could defeat you by looking at you or blowing at you; a hero who could push the world around by doing handstands. Marvel's heroes had been more down-to-earth; bringing in someone of godly abilities would enable them to do Superman-level stories.

Lee said in an interview, "Now I'm not the world's greatest authority on gods, so I brushed up on the Roman gods, and I said, 'Awww, we've seen a lot of them.' Looked into the Greek gods and, well, everybody knows them. And then I stumbled on the Norse gods. And I thought, *they're not as well known.* So I was reading about them and I came across the mighty Thor, God of Thunder. And I liked the idea of it: that he could create storms; that he was one of the strongest if not the strongest of all the Norse gods."

He was also, as it turned out, something of a hell-raiser.

Thor, in the Marvel version, was not the son of Frigga. Instead, thanks to Odin's desire to have a son whose power would derive from both Midgard as well as Asgard, Odin wound up mating with Gaea, the spirit of the planet—Mother Earth, if you will—in the guise of "Jord." Thor was born in an Odin-created cave in Norway, and once the infant thunder god was weaned, Odin took him to Asgard where he was raised believing that Odin's wife, Frigga, was his mother.

As the young thunder god grew up, he was active in both worlds of his heritage.

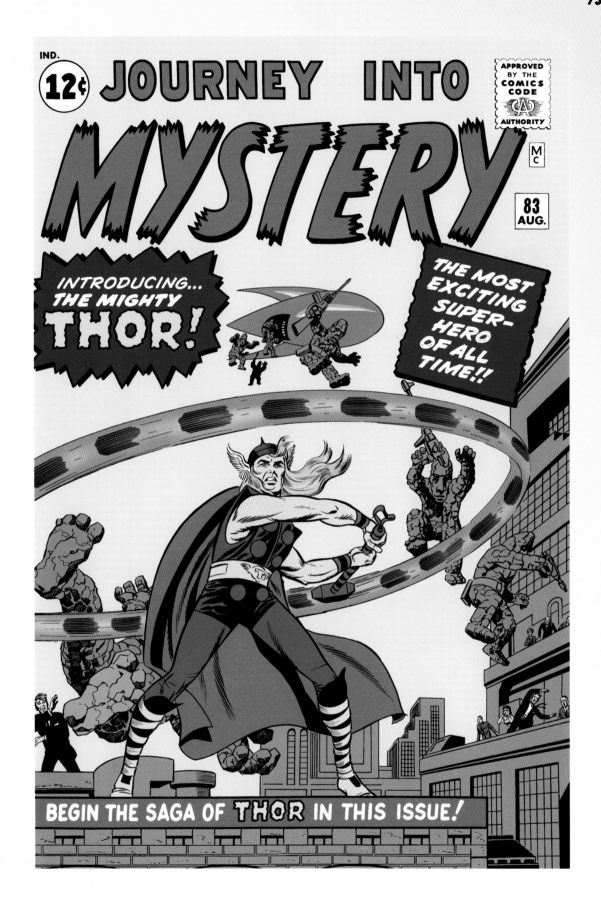

ABOVE: Thor debuted in *Journey into Mystery #83*. His first battle was against the Stone Men from Saturn. Art by Jack Kirby and Joe Sinnott.

BEHOLD IN BREATHLESS WONDER, THE GOD OF THUNDER, MIGHTY THOR

was a busy god. Unfortunately those stories exacerbated a quickly escalating continuity snafu that had its roots in the story that launched Thor in the first place.

RAISING CANE

In *Journey into Mystery #83*, readers were introduced to Donald Blake, a lame doctor who was on holiday in Norway. During his time there, he ran into that huge inconvenience that all tourists just hate: invading Stone Men from Saturn. Inadvertently attracting their attention, he fled into a cave that, unbeknownst to him, had served as the birthplace of a young god millennia ago. In the process he lost his cane, but he discovered a long stick that would, in a pinch, serve as a substitute. In a moment of frustration he whacked the wall with the cane. Lightning struck and he discovered himself transformed into Fabio with a winged helmet. The cane itself had become a hammer, and on the head of the

Something of a peoples' god, he took delight in fighting alongside the Vikings and basking in their adulation. However, at one point he discovered that some of his followers had slaughtered the inhabitants of a Christian monastery, purportedly in his name. Appalled that the massacre of harmless individuals was carried out on his behalf, Thor departed Earth. It was the beginning of the end of the active worship of Asgardians.

Which wasn't to say that Thor didn't have enough to keep him occupied in Asgard and its environs. Between various quests and adventures—described in such sources as the back-up series "Tales of Asgard"—Thor

ABOVE: Donald Blake, taking refuge in a cave from the Stone Men, happens upon a cane that turns out to be much more than it appears. Art by Jack Kirby and Joe Sinnott.

ABOVE: The cover for *Thor #6,* by Olivier Coipel and Mark Morales.

THE CAVE IS BATHED IN BLINDING LIGHT..!! LIKE A FIERY BOLT OF LIGHTNING..! AND THE ANCIENT CANE--IT--**IT'S CHANGING SHAPE!**

AND--**I'M** CHANGING **TOO..!!**

CAN THIS BE REALLY **HAPPENING** --OR AM I GOING **MAD?!!**

NO! IT ISN'T MAD..!! I CAN FEEL MY BODY BURSTING WITH **POWER-- POWER** SUCH AS I'VE NEVER KNOWN..!!

THE CANE..!! IT HAS BECOME A MIGHTY **HAMMER..!!** AND **I** HAVE BEEN TRANSFORMED INTO--INTO--**WAIT!** THERE ARE **WORDS** INSCRIBED ON THE HAMMER..!!

"**WHOSOEVER HOLDS THIS HAMMER**, IF HE BE **WORTHY**, SHALL **POSSESS THE POWER OF...** **THOR**"

THOR..!! THE LEGENDARY GOD OF **THUNDER..!!** THE MIGHTIEST WARRIOR OF ALL MYTHOLOGY..!! THIS IS **HIS** HAMMER..!! AND I--**I AM THOR..!!!**

For those readers who might not have heard of him, the newly transformed Blake declared, "Thor! The legendary god of Thunder! The mightiest warrior of all mythology! This is his hammer! And I . . . I am Thor!"

He wasn't just Thor. He was pissed off. He quickly routed the Stone Men, sending them scampering back to Saturn and saving the entire Earth . . . and that was just in his debut!

The issue also featured a detective story, "The Perfect Crime," and the unlikely tale of an irradiated lion

hammer was the following grammatically debatable inscription: "Whosoever holds this hammer, if he be worthy, shall possess the power of Thor!"

that almost conquers the world called "When the Jungle Sleeps."

Despite being a god, Thor wasn't exempt from the usual super hero tropes.

ABOVE: Thor's first appearance in *Journey into Mystery #83*. Art by Jack Kirby and Joe Sinnott.

Donald Blake was not only his secret identity but also his weakness. The "holds this hammer" inscription was literal: If the hammer was out of Thor's hand for more than sixty seconds, he transformed back into the helpless Blake, while Mjolnir reverted to a cane . . . or remained a hammer, depending upon the story requirements and Lee's memory.

His other weakness, so to speak, was for his nurse, Jane Foster, who was hopelessly in love with him. But Jane was unaware of both Blake's alter ego and, naturally, the fact that Odin absolutely forbade his son's involvement with a mortal. These things would create major friction and romantic tension.

A year or so after Thor arrived on the scene, "Tales of Asgard" debuted, and in short order, fans were asking a fairly reasonable question: Where was Thor before Donald Blake found the hammer? The answer didn't come until 1968. When it did, it was one of the earliest examples of retcon.

ABOVE: Cover art for *Tales of Asgard* ran as a popular backup feature of *Journey into Mystery*. This one-shot reprinted stories from issues #97–#106. Adapted from an original Jack Kirby illustration.

In a story appropriately entitled, "The Answer at Last!" in *The Mighty Thor #159*, Donald Blake dreamt of going to Asgard as Thor to find the answer to the same question that the fans had been asking. Odin, uncharacteristically obliging, showed up in Blake's apartment and gave a brilliantly simple explanation.

It seemed that Thor's brashness and arrogance had reached a tipping point. First Thor chased a birdbeast across a border into Niffleheim, violating a truce and triggering such a confrontation with the resident giants that his oldest friend, Balder, had to rescue him. Thor then wound up in a tavern where a simple arm-wrestling contest led to a massive bar brawl that required the intervention of Odin himself.

Fed up with cleaning up after his son's messes, Odin banished him to Earth, wiped out his memory of his true nature, and provided him with a human identity as a doctor. He would spend his days tending to the needs of the sick and helpless, and also be lame of leg himself, thus instilling in Odin's wayward son an appreciation for those who were weaker than he. (We later learned that his desire to visit Norway, and his discovery of that particular cave where the disguised Mjolnir were resting, were courtesy of a little mental nudging on Odin's part. Whether Odin also thought it would be a good idea to up the jeopardy by sending in the Stone Men of Saturn remains unknown.)

In one brilliant stroke Lee and Kirby covered the continuity train wreck of "Tales of Asgard," and even explained why Donald Blake's relationship with Jane Foster (which had ended in an earlier issue) was doomed to failure. There was never an option of Donald Blake choosing between being mortal and being Thor: He *was* Thor, and always had been.

STOP! HAMMER TIME

It's worth devoting a bit of space to Thor's distinctive weapon, so famed that ancient (and modern) pieces of jewelry are based upon it.

According to Stan Lee, he "especially liked the idea that Thor had a hammer. I figured, 'What a weapon!' It's not a gun, it's not a knife. A hammer! I'm lucky it wasn't a screwdriver, or it could have been a pair of pliers. But I think a hammer is really dramatic. Now, I want to show you how scientific we were at Marvel Comics. We needed

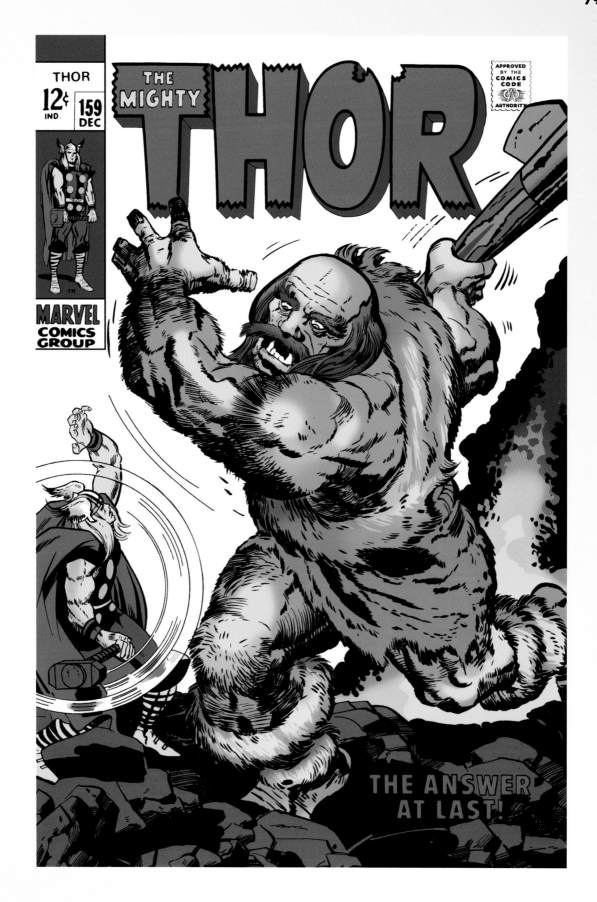

ABOVE: The historic *Mighty Thor #159* explains Thor's true origin. Art by Jack Kirby and Vince Colletta.

BEHOLD IN BREATHLESS WONDER, THE GOD OF THUNDER, MIGHTY THOR

SWINGING HIS ENCHANTED MALLET, AND HOLDING FAST TO THE UNBREAKABLE THONG, THE MIGHTY THOR TAKES TO THE AIR!

a method for Thor to fly so that he could go from Asgard to the Earth. I didn't want him to just say, 'I think I'll get going' and bingo, we see him fly. If you ever thought about it, Superman flies with no visible means of propulsion. I wanted Thor to have a real method of flying. So I figured, he'll take his hammer and [attach] a little leather thong and wrap it around his wrist. And then he'll swing the hammer very fast like a propeller. And when it gets going at top speed, he'll let it go! Now the hammer will go flying off, but since the thong is tied to his wrist, it'll pull him along with it. So you see, everything I ever wrote was scientifically sound!"

In Thor's personal Marvel chronology, Mjolnir first showed up when he was eight years old. Odin dispatched him to Nidavellir, the land of the dwarfs, with a message for two dwarfs named Brokk and Eitri: They were to craft three treasures for him. One of the three treasures was a war hammer made of a metal called Uru that was nigh indestructible, not acquiring so much as a ding over the years until an Odin-created killer robot called the Destroyer rather shockingly split the hammer head in half with a ray blast in *Journey into Mystery #118.* (Thor would repair his hammer two issues later in the fires of a foundry in Pittsburgh.) The dwarfs used the heart of a star as a mold, blowing up the star and nearly annihilating Midgard in the process.

Odin put several enchantments upon the hammer, not the least of which was that only someone who was truly worthy would be able to wield it. (As opposed

---

ABOVE: Thor doesn't actually have the power to fly; he simply throws the hammer and then grabs the strap and hangs on as it pulls him through the air, shown here in *Journey into Mystery #97.* Art by Jack Kirby and Don Heck.

ABOVE: The Destroyer manages what no one else can: He shatters Mjolnir in this momentous scene in *Journey into Mystery #118*. Art by Jack Kirby and Vince Colletta.

BEHOLD IN BREATHLESS WONDER, THE GOD OF THUNDER, MIGHTY THOR

to the original conceit that it was simply too damned heavy.) Weight, however, does play a factor since the Hulk was once depicted as actually being able to lift the hammer through sheer muscle power, even if only a couple of inches, and one would be hard-pressed to deem the Hulk worthy.

The length of Mjolnir's handle fluctuated initially, depending upon the artist. Sometimes the hammer was depicted looking somewhat like a croquet mallet. Eventually it was stated in the Letters page that the hammer's handle was a foot in length, probably because it was easier to remember, and the visual has remained consistent since.

Typically the hammer returns to Thor, although in rare instances heavy-duty electronics (such as robots) have been able to stop it. It's always been assumed that the hammer simply does so because of an enchantment, although on at least one occasion, Thor has been shown summoning the weapon by whispering its "real name," whatever that may be.

The hammer was the device by which Thor was able to transform into and out of his Donald Blake persona, changing shape itself in the process to the simple cane (which could be lifted by anybody). Mjolnir focused Thor's weather-changing powers, helping him create everything from lightning to deluges, from tornadoes to tidal waves, from earthquakes to volcanoes. Aptly enough, anything that can be termed an act of God can be cooked up by Thor's hammer.

At various times, Thor has used the hammer for other miscellaneous purposes, including some one-off effects that basically serve the story needs. Among Mjolnir's properties:

- Channeling the God Blast, a focused unleashing of all Thor's godly energies that was so potent it actually shattered the hammer;
- Releasing the Anti-Force, a blast so powerful that it can shatter a planet (so you don't really want to use that too much if you're standing on Earth)—not to be confused with the equally planet-shattering power of the Thermo Blast;
- The ability to transmute elements;
- Deflecting anything heading Thor's way, from bullets to energy blasts;
- The ability to open up portals through space and even through

ABOVE: In *Journey into Mystery #112*—an insert of *Avengers #3*—Thor recounts a prolonged battle with the Hulk. Here the Hulk, for one of the few times in his life, is able to wield the hammer. Art by Jack Kirby and Chic Stone.

 BEHOLD IN BREATHLESS WONDER, THE GOD OF THUNDER, MIGHTY THOR

time, although the latter power was eventually dispensed with;

- Being lethal to the undead since it's a religious icon. This was demonstrated when a vampire, struck by Mjolnir, burst into flame and crumbled to dust. Of course, since Mjolnir could easily decapitate a vampire, the added benefits of this particular ability are dubious at best.

THE WARRIORS THREE

Agent Garrett: Is there a Renaissance Faire in town?

Agent Jackson: Call it in.

Agent Garrett: Yeah, uh, base? We've got, uh, Xena, Jackie Chan, and Robin Hood.

—Two S.H.I.E.L.D. agents reacting to the arrival of Sif, Hogun, and Fandral in the 2011 film *Thor*

Journey into Mystery #119 was a momentous issue. It introduced Fandral the Dashing, Hogun the Grim, and Volstagg the Vast, collectively known as the Warriors Three, Thor's heroic trio of sidekicks. Although they are described as

gods of Asgard, unlike Thor, they are not based on any Norse myths. Indeed, one might conjecture that they are instead warriors of different eras, plucked from their deaths by the Valkyries and brought to Valhalla, the hall of warriors, to spend eternity in endless and glorious combat.

One is rarely seen without the other two, and the adjectives that usually follow their names pretty much cover their major attributes. All three of them are utterly devoted to Thor and would be willing to—and indeed, have—followed him into the gates of Hel.

Fandral the Dashing appears to have been mostly inspired by Errol Flynn, with rakish blond hair and a beard that could only be described as, well, dashing. He is a master swordsman, and is something of a womanizer (albeit not quite as successful as he seems to claim or at least believe). He even boasted once of having married an Earth woman named Marian, suggesting (although not confirming) that he was indeed the basis for Robin Hood.

Hogun the Grim is the polar opposite of Fandral. Dressed in a manner vaguely

ABOVE: Cover art for *The Warriors Three #1*, a four-issue limited series in which Thor's heroic trio of sidekicks Hogun, Volstagg, and Fandral battle a creature unleashed from the depths of Hel. Art by Salvador Espin.

BEHOLD IN BREATHLESS WONDER, THE GOD OF THUNDER, MIGHTY THOR

evocative of a Mongol, Hogun was, according to Stan Lee, based somewhat on actor Charles Bronson. He's the most taciturn of the group—indeed, of pretty much every god in Asgard—although he does have a fiery temper. His weapon of choice is a large mace, Hridgandr, which he wields with deadly accuracy and effect (although he has also been known to use a sword). Hogun has little patience with Fandral's devil-may-care attitude, but nevertheless respects his prowess and always has his back.

Volstagg the Vast, a.k.a. the Lion of Asgard (a nickname he is wont to apply to himself; others rarely do), is easily the most developed of the three. With a vaguely Elizabethan look that evokes comparisons to Shakespeare's Falstaff (as do the similarities of name), Volstagg was initially there for comic relief. He was largely (no pun intended) a coward, seeking to avoid fights while loudly proclaiming that he was at the forefront of the battle. Over time, though, Volstagg became disgusted by his own fears and put his formidable battle skills to work, although mostly they involved throwing his weight around to formidable effect. Volstagg is also the only member of the three to have a family: a wife, four daughters, and four sons (two of them adopted).

Sif is not one of the Warriors Three, obviously, but an important goddess of Asgard and in Thor's life. A formidable warrior, she has been Thor's staunch

ABOVE: The Warriors Three, depicted in *Thor #368.* Art by Vince Colletta.

companion and astound-
ingly understanding and
patient love interest.

Sif first appeared
in *Journey into Mystery
#102* in "Tales of Asgard:
Death Comes to Thor."
Introduced as the younger
sister of Heimdall, the
guardian of Bifrost, Sif
had to be saved from the
clutches of the Storm
Giants by Thor. Thor
went on to have some-
thing of an on-again,
off-again relationship with
her. Her major entrance
into the ongoing continu-
ity was in *The Mighty Thor
#136*, and it could not
have been better timed.
Odin, finally warming to
Jane Foster, had brought
her to Asgard so that she
could be made into a goddess and marry
Thor. But the challenges were simply too
much for her as she wailed, like Alice at
the tea party, "I don't want it! I won't be
a goddess! I won't stay in Asgard! It's too

horrible! Too unendurable! Don't you realize how mad it is?!"

Odin promptly erased her memory of
Asgard and returned her to Earth. This infuriated Thor, who threatened to go after her.

ABOVE: Sif pictured on the cover of issue #3 of *Thor: Son of Asgard,* an epic coming-of-age story. Art by Adi Granov.

about two pages before running into Sif for the first time in ages and suddenly it was, "Jane Who?" Which was, of course, what Odin was expecting.

FAMILY ISSUES

It's safe to say that although many heroes in the Marvel Universe had difficulties with members of their families, none of them had to deal with the level of sheer dysfunction that Thor had to cope with month after month. With Thor's adopted mom, Frigga, more or less absent, Thor was constantly caught between the machina-

Odin, giving him the biggest "Told you so" in the history of comics, verbally smacked Thor down and sent him on patrol to cool off. Thor, who had been pining for Jane Foster for five years, mourned the loss for

tions of his adopted brother, Loki, and the extremely short leash Odin kept him on.

As the boss of bosses, Odin was concerned with the smooth running of his realm. As a father who apparently had zero respect

---

ABOVE: Thor meets Sif in *Thor #136* and falls for her only a few pages after losing his beloved Jane Foster. Art by Jack Kirby and Vince Colletta.

THE AVENGERS VAULT

for his son's choices, Odin was obsessed with spying on his offspring and bringing him into line with a proper immortal life. And he had the power to back up his judgments: physically the strongest of all the immortals of Asgard, Odin could also make his anger known to Thor by punishing his wayward son—typically by robbing him of some portion of his power at the worst possible time, such as in the middle of a battle.

Odin also wielded the Odin Power, a.k.a. the Odin Force, a boundless internal fount of energy that he could manipulate pretty much any way he wanted, ranging from unleashing force blasts to transporting the entire human race to another planet. Indeed, it must have been a bit frustrating that he could do whatever he desired except bend Thor to his will. His power, though, wasn't endless: every so often he needed to effectively recharge by taking a power nap called the Odinsleep. (He was big on putting "Odin-" in front

ABOVE: The All-Father exercising his might in *Thor #158*. Art by Jack Kirby and Vince Colletta.

ABOVE: *The Mighty Thor #274* is part of a story line where the gods face the realities of Ragnarok. Balder dies just as the legends claim he will, and Odin winds up losing an eye. Art by John Buscema and Tom Palmer.

of just about everything connected to him; apparently having a day of the week named after him just wasn't enough.)

In *The Mighty Thor #274*, Odin sacrificed an eye in order to try and avert Ragnarok, thus bringing him visually into line with his original mythological counterpart.

Odin displayed something of a blind spot toward his son Loki. Thor occasionally referred to Loki as his half-brother. He was in fact Odin's adopted son, the offspring of the giant Laufey, whom Odin slew in combat. In the original mythology Loki was himself a giant and a trickster who enjoyed pulling pranks on the gods, occasionally with lethal results. In the Marvel version, Loki was the same size as any of the other Asgardians, and was far more malevolent than his mythic counterpart. Nowhere near Thor's power level in strength, he compensated with mastery of sorcery, which he used constantly to both attack Thor directly and through cat's paws that would do his dirty work for him.

His first appearance in a comic was actually back in 1949, when he crossed

---

ABOVE: Although Loki first showed up in a Golden Age story many years earlier, he made his Marvel Age debut in the pages of *Journey into Mystery #85*. Art by Jack Kirby and Dick Ayers.

ABOVE: The cover of *Journey into Mystery #85*. Art by Jack Kirby and Dick Ayers.

mythologies and showed up to harass the goddess Venus, who found herself "Face to Face with the King of Evil" in the sixth issue of her own title. He was depicted with a flat-topped head and orange hair, and was inexplicably ruling the underworld of Roman mythology. His return in the modern era was *Journey into Mystery #85*, a mere two issues after Thor's debut. Odin had, at some point, gotten fed up with him—possibly because he was posing as a Roman god in 1949—and trapped him inside a tree. Loki, appropriately, tricked his way free of his imprisonment and showed that he hadn't learned his lesson by immediately going to Earth, causing a panic, and attacking Thor.

That same issue also featured the first appearance of Asgard and such luminaries as Odin, Balder, Heimdall, and Tyr.

From that point on, Loki would continually harass and plot against his brother. Most of the time, though, he stopped short of actually trying to kill his enemy, fearing the wrath of Odin should something terminal happen to Thor (oddly displaying more worry over Thor's life than Thor's own father did). Yet despite the fact that Loki was relentlessly evil while Thor's only sin was that he loved unwisely, Odin would occasionally trust Loki over Thor, even leaving him in charge on occasion, which predictably led to disaster.

Loki has gone through various permutations through the years, including being a female for a while and currently an adolescent, but during all that time his/her ultimate goal has remained grasping power and making Thor's life difficult. Interestingly, that rivalry resulted in the creation of the Avengers—in both the films and the comic books. So for all the evil he's done, perhaps Loki can be given a measure of forgiveness since he was responsible for bringing together the greatest fighting team in the history of the world.

But probably not.

GOD OF TWO WORLDS

Thor's initial stay on Earth was fraught with deep personal struggle. At first, Donald Blake was simply a guy with the power of . . . Thor. But then Odin showed up—and it was all downhill from there.

Of particular interest to Odin was Thor's involvement with Jane Foster. Thor's romatic problem was the reverse of the famous Superman triangle, in that Jane loved his mortal half and didn't have any particular

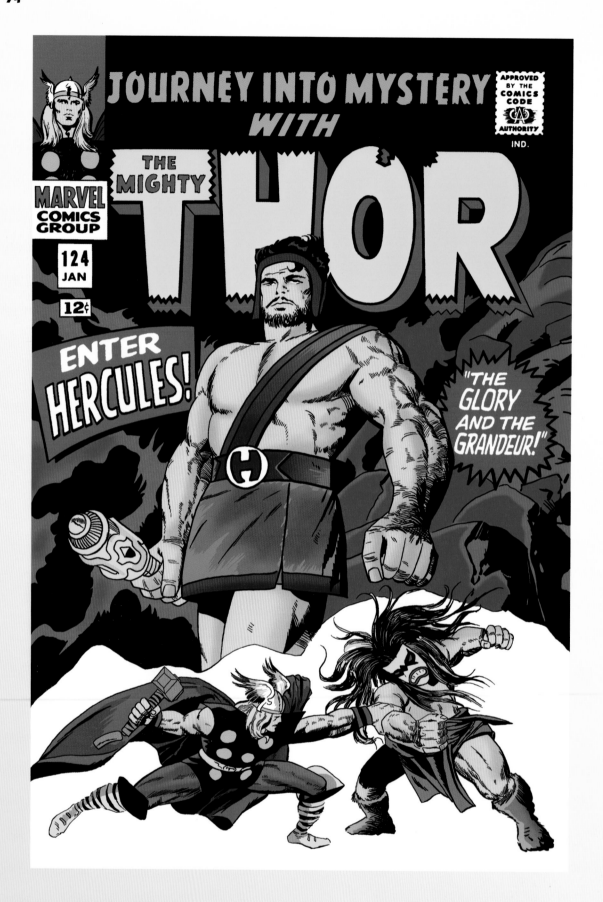

ABOVE: *Journey into Mystery #124* covers major events in Thor's life as he reveals his identity to Jane Foster and battles Hercules. Art by Jack Kirby and Vince Colletta.

interest in Thor. But Donald constantly had to make excuses for his absences while Odin simultaneously scolded Thor for his interest in Jane and occasionally punished him by halving his powers or some such. Finally, Thor became fed up with the duplicity and, frustrated over Jane's depression about their relationship, revealed his identity to Jane in *Journey into Mystery #124.* He then promptly got put in his place by Hercules. It was always something of a 50/50 proposition whether Thor was concerned about the Earth. In point of fact, it really depended on whoever happened to be writing the series at the time. Those who preferred Thor adventuring in Asgard or fantasy realms would do stories set there, while others felt he was better served on Earth, sometimes hanging out with the Avengers.

DOCTOR WHO?

Dr. Blake has not been Thor's only human incarnation.

ERIC MASTERSON

Eric was an architect who first showed up in *The Mighty Thor #391.* Pulled into the thunder god's orbit, Eric was initially crippled and then nearly killed by various super villains including the Mongoose. With Eric on the brink of death, Thor wound up merging himself with Eric so that Eric effectively

ABOVE: Donald Blake reveals the secret of his double life to Jane Foster, a revelation with major consequences. Art by Jack Kirby and Vince Colletta.

became his new human identity. This lasted for a while until they were separated, then briefly remerged, then separated again. Upon that second separation, Eric was made over into an incarnation of Thor and served as the thunder god on Earth for a time, wielding Mjolnir and working with the Avengers. Eventually Thor took his hammer back and Odin presented Eric with a new weapon, a mace called Thunderstrike. This, however, did not work out all that well for Eric in the long term as he was eventually killed and sent off into the afterlife after passing up the opportunity to lounge in Valhalla.

SIGURD JARLSON

When the alien Beta Ray Bill came along, Odin transferred the transmuting power of the hammer into Bill's weapon. This knocked the Donald Blake persona out of existence, and, with Nick Fury's aid, Thor took on the secret identity of construction worker Sigurd Jarlson. He basically looked pretty much like himself; he just wore glasses and tied his hair back in a ponytail. Because everyone knows that when you wear glasses and your hair differently, no one can tell you're a super hero.

JAKE OLSON

Jake worked as an EMT but moonlighted as a thief and drug dealer. He wound up being killed in an explosion, and when his grieving girlfriend went to his apartment to clean out his stuff, she was shocked to find that he was there, hale and hardy. Except not really: he was actually Thor, who had been placed within a human identity to help hide him from the Dark Gods, some Asgardian enemies with whom he was at war at the time. Loki wound up restoring Jake to life and eventually the two of them—the real Jake and Thor/Jake—wound up slugging it out in a convenience store. When real Jake was knocked out, Loki stepped in and took over the body, sending Jake's soul screaming off to hell. But Loki was then stuck in Jake's body, rendering him mortal, and he wound up in jail.

"IF HE BE WORTHY"

In 1983, Marvel released a widely circulated flier/ad featuring the question, "What have they done to the mighty Thor?" The accompanying illustration, rather than being the long-haired warrior, was something that looked like a two-legged horse, defiantly wielding Mjolnir.

ABOVE: For a time, Thor assumes the identity of Sigurd Jarlson. Unlike the body-shifting transformation to Donald Blake, Jarlson was just a bearded Thor with glasses and his hair tied back. Art by Sal Buscema and Christie Scheele.

BEHOLD IN BREATHLESS WONDER, THE GOD OF THUNDER, MIGHTY THOR

ABOVE: *Thor #337* includes the thunder god's first encounter with Beta Ray Bill—an adversary so worthy, he is able to lift Thor's hammer and acquire its power. Art by Walt Simonson and George Roussos.

This individual had the unlikely name of Beta Ray Bill. Bill was the defender of a severely depleted race called the Korbonites, whose galaxy had been thoroughly messed up by the fire demon, Surtur. When their fleeing vessel was detected by S.H.I.E.L.D., Nick Fury asked Thor to check into it. Thor did so and wound up in a battle with Bill, during which Thor was separated from Mjolnir for more than sixty seconds—returning him to Donald Blake. Blake was knocked unconscious and Bill, finding the fallen Mjolnir, touched it out of curiosity. This triggered the inscription "Whosoever holds this hammer, *if he be worthy,* shall possess the power of Thor." Apparently Bill was worthy enough, and he suddenly found himself powered up.

How did Odin sort this mess out? Naturally he had the two of them battle it out on a planet that, due to its volcanic composition, gave the advantage to Bill who wound up defeating Thor yet again. But Bill refused to kill the thunder god, and as a reward for his gallantry, Odin—returning Mjolnir to Thor—created a new hammer for Bill called Stormbreaker.

Bill went on to a series of adventures of his own, his interests usually crossing with those of Thor. He also had several miniseries. Eventually he wound up with the Annihilators, a cosmic team designed to replace the then-fallen Guardians of the Galaxy.

BAD GUYS, PART TWO

Although all of the Avengers have an array of interesting foes, Thor's are by far the most out of this world. From underground to outer space, from other times and other dimensions, Thor's foes span the entirety of existence.

THE ABSORBING MAN

Crusher Creel, a boxer and career criminal, was transformed into the new identity of the Absorbing Man in *Journey into Mystery #114* when Loki whipped up a potion that gave him the power to duplicate the properties of whatever he touched. If he gripped metal, for instance, he became a man of metal. Which technically makes him more of a duplicating man than an absorbing man since he doesn't actually absorb the object's properties. His primary weapon is a ball and chain that likewise duplicates objects' properties. He is formidable in a battle, unless he can be tricked into touching glass, in which case he is extremely vulnerable.

revealed). He was initially employed by Loki (again) to take down the god of thunder, and in his first outing came closer than just about anyone else. The Destroyer actually managed to cut Mjolnir in half with a force beam, and the only thing that saved Thor's life was Loki suddenly realizing that if the Destroyer did indeed kill Thor, Odin would come looking for payback and the trail would lead straight to Loki himself. So at the point where the Destroyer had Thor imprisoned in the ground, Loki—imprisoned in his cell in Asgard—used magic to make him intangible and thus enabled him to escape. Then Thor managed to bury the Destroyer under a literal mountain of rock, and that ended the threat for the moment.

THE DESTROYER

First showing up in *Journey into Mystery #118*, the Destroyer is essentially a sentient suit of armor created by Odin to defend against a menace from the stars (the Celestials, as it would eventually be

The Destroyer has shown up again several times since then, and it's always been a tough battle for Thor. He also fought against Thor in the first feature film, once again dispatched by Loki to do in the thunder

---

ABOVE: The cover of *Journey into Mystery #118* in which Thor first encounters the Destroyer. Art by Jack Kirby and Vince Colletta.

god. He came close, but the newly repowered Thor pretty much blew him away with the power of the storm.

THE ENCHANTRESS AND THE EXECUTIONER

These two Asgardians have done significant damage to each other in their time, but in the early days they tended to operate as a team.

Skurge was a heavily muscled Asgardian who went by the name "Executioner," and supplemented that name by wielding a massive battle axe. Hopelessly in love with the Enchantress, he was usually tangled up in whatever her latest scheme was to rain hell down on Thor. Eventually, however, Skurge's loyalties wound up swinging over to the other side and he sacrificed his life in a massive battle designed to delay Ragnarok. He was subsequently welcomed into Valhalla as a hero.

The Enchantress, whose real name is Amora, is a formidable Asgardian sorceress. For her first mission, which Skurge joined her for, she was to get rid of Jane Foster, because that's just how much Odin despised the poor mortal woman. They

ABOVE: In *Journey into Mystery #103*, Odin decides the best way to get Thor's mind off Jane Foster is to send in the Enchantress. Not one of his better moves. Art by Jack Kirby and Chic Stone.

didn't succeed, and Odin, displaying his famed mercy, banished them to Earth.

Throughout her career the Enchantress tended to switch sides until eventually, long after the Jane Foster days, she became Thor's lover and they cohabited in a New York City apartment. She was later slain during one of the Asgardians' go-rounds with Ragnarok.

HELA

The daughter of Loki, Hela is the goddess who rules over the Norse death realms of Hel and Niffleheim. She is one of Thor's most formidable enemies—her very touch means death.

Her dustups with Thor have been legendary. Most memorably, she once cursed him with the inability to die while simultaneously rendering his bones extremely fragile so that every battle did untold damage to him. She has also tried to expand her power on occasion, with an eye on Valhalla, the realm of undead warriors.

Much of Hela's powers stem from her cloak. A tall, statuesque woman while wearing the cloak, without it her body reverts into something that is half gorgeous and half withered.

MALEKITH THE ACCURSED

Blue-skinned, long-haired, with a split black-and-white face, Malekith is the ruler of the Dark Elves of Svartalfheim. A formidable fighter and possessor of various psychic abilities as well, Malekith was determined to unleash a permanent frozen winter upon the Earth. Thor obviously had something to say about this. Malekith was supposedly slain during his early outings, but was later revealed to be alive.

SURTUR

Taken straight from Norse mythology, Surtur the Fire Demon has been a major thorn in Thor's side since *Journey into Mystery #97* back in 1963. A resident of the extradimensional plane of Muspelheim, Surtur will torch the world after the fighting of Ragnarok is done, according to Norse mythology.

As tall as an average skyscraper, Surtur has massive power, much of it naturally tied in with flame. He has attempted to invade Earth and destroy it several times. The first attempt, he wound up in a slugfest with Odin and Thor, with Odin taking the precaution of transporting every human being into an alternate dimension so that the globe-spanning

ABOVE: *The Mighty Thor #345* introduces Malekith, the Dark Elf, who will plague Thor repeatedly over the years. Art by Walt Simonson and Christie Scheele.

BEHOLD IN BREATHLESS WONDER, THE GOD OF THUNDER, MIGHTY THOR

especially when those times have to do with Ragnarok.

ULIK THE TROLL

If your image of a troll is a little guy who hides under a bridge and spouts riddles, then you've never met a rock troll. Ulik is one of the most formidable of that species, which reside in Nornheim and spend most of their free time hating Odin for having banished them underground.

Initially Ulik is instructed by the king of the rock trolls to steal Mjolnir to simplify a planned invasion of Asgard. Ulik makes a good fight of it, but ultimately fails in the endeavor.

Ulik would repeatedly return over the years to harass Thor and his allies. For a time during which it was believed that Thor

battle wouldn't take any innocents with it. Thor eventually managed to trap Surtur inside a meteorite in another dimension.

He broke free and has managed to make life difficult for Thor from time to time,

---

ABOVE: Thor squares off against the Lava Man in *Journey into Mystery #97*. Art by Jack Kirby and Don Heck.

was dead, Ulik even took his place, recreating himself as Tanarus, the new god of thunder. Fortunately, his own belligerent disposition and temper made it evident that something was amiss, and Thor, upon his return, defeated the troll.

AVENGERS VS. GODS VS. AVENGERS

Eventually one of the Ragnaroks in Thor's history wound up taking out Asgard and all the gods. But nothing keeps a god down, not even death. Thor eventually bounced back and wound up rebuilding Asgard as a floating city above, of all places, Broxton, Oklahoma. He then spent his time retrieving the Asgardians who had wound

up on Earth in other identities. He was also somewhat annoyed to discover the details of the Marvel Civil War and was particularly steamed to learn that Tony Stark had crafted a clone of him to serve by his side.

And then Norman Osborn decided that Asgard posed a threat to his plans, so he contended that it was a threat to national security and received permission to invade the floating city. Thor wound up falling in battle, but these actions so infuriated Captain America that he and his team of Avengers—not to mention another team called the Avengers Resistance—entered

---

ABOVE: *Thor #137* features Thor's first battle against Ulik, the mightiest of the rock trolls. Art by Jack Kirby and Vince Colletta.

BEHOLD IN BREATHLESS WONDER, THE GOD OF THUNDER, MIGHTY THOR

find the thunder god in the simple act of walking around town. The New York citizenry are duly impressed. And then a little girl tells Thor how her dad is off fighting in Vietnam and Thor kneels down and embraces her. The crowd coos over his coddling of the child.

That was how Thor was viewed in the old days. People accepted the concept that a mythic god was walking among them and were mostly impressed by him.

More modern-day renderings have taken a closer and even more skeptical look at his godly status. (The Asgardians of the films are aliens, not gods.) Meanwhile in recent retroactive stories that attempt to retell the Avengers' origins with modern-day sensibilities, Tony Stark has openly expressed skepticism that Thor is who and what he says he is. A being of immense power? No doubt. But a god? A ridiculous notion.

However Thor is regarded—true god or merely a powerful imposter—there is no doubt he remains one of the foremost figures in the Marvel Universe.

the fray in order to try and set things right.

At the end of the story line, entitled "Siege," Asgard was knocked out of the sky, but Osborn fell from power and the entire Super Hero Registration Act was discontinued.

THOR, THE ROCK GOD OF GODS

In one issue of *Journey into Mystery*, we

ABOVE: The cover of *The Ultimates #4*. Art by Brian Hitch, Andrew Currie, and Paul Mounts.

ENCLOSED 1: A 1985 poster promoting Thunder Frog (a.k.a. Throg). Art by Walt Simonson.

ENCLOSED 2: An original color guide from *Avengers #309*. Art by Paul Ryan, Tom Palmer, and Christie Scheele.

4

YOU'VE GOTTA
HAVE HEART

Reporter: "Mr. Stark, you've been called the Da Vinci of our time. What do you say to that?"

Stark: "Absolutely ridiculous. I don't paint."

—*IRON MAN*

TONY STARK IS, OF COURSE, EXACTLY THAT. LACK OF painting ability notwithstanding, the only other individual who is on par with Stark's knack for invention is Reed Richards, and even Reed might take himself out of the running.

Stark made his first appearance in *Tales of Suspense #39*. Stan Lee once described his creation thusly: "I thought—I don't

OPPOSITE: Iron Man, ready for action.

ABOVE: Iron Man made his debut in *Tales of Suspense #39*. Art by Jack Kirby, Don Heck, and Stan Goldberg.

know why I thought it, somebody in a suit of armor. And what if it was iron armor. He would be so powerful. So for some reason I have always been fascinated by Howard Hughes. I thought I would get a hero like Howard Hughes. He's an inventor. He's a multimillionaire. He's good looking. He likes the women. But I've got to make something tragic about him."

YES, ANTHONY STARK IS BOTH A SOPHISTICATE AND A SCIENTIST! A MILLIONAIRE BACHELOR, AS MUCH AT HOME IN A LABORATORY AS IN HIGH SOCIETY!

BUT, THIS MAN WHO SEEMS SO FORTUNATE, WHO'S ENVIED BY MILLIONS -- IS SOON DESTINED TO BECOME THE MOST TRAGIC FIGURE ON EARTH!

He went on to state, in an interview conducted by ABDO Publishing, "Iron Man's appeal . . . stems from a few things. One is the fact that he has an injured heart, so no matter how strong his armor is he's still always very vulnerable. Then two, he's wealthy and not uncomfortable with that fact. I think most readers would want to be as wealthy as Tony. Of course, the fact that he's handsome and glamorous endears him to the hearts of many female readers. Finally, he actually has no super power

of his own—only his fantastic armor; and without that armor he's just as human as any of his readers."

What was Stan's inspiration for Iron Man's alter ego? In an interview connected to the DVD release of *Iron Man*, he stated, "I think I gave myself a dare. It was the height of the Cold War. The readers, the young readers, if there was one thing they hated, it was war, it was the military. So I got a hero who represented that to the hundredth degree. He was a weapons manufacturer, he was providing weapons for the

ABOVE: In *Tales of Suspense #39*, Tony Stark is kidnapped, triggering the sequence of events that leads to the creation of the armored Avenger. Art by Jack Kirby, Don Heck, and Stan Goldberg.

Army, he was rich, he was an industrialist. I thought it would be fun to take the kind of character that nobody would like, none of our readers would like, and shove him down their throats and make them like him . . . And he became very popular."

The specifics of Stark's origin were tied into the Vietnam War, which, as the years passed, was retconned first to the Gulf War, and then Afghanistan. Stark, the adopted son of genius Howard Stark, is blown up by a booby trap, becoming the prisoner of a terrorist who wants him to create weapons for him. Stark works in conjunction with another captured scientist, Yinsen, but the two men are actually scheming to make a break for it by crafting a formidable weapon: an armor made of iron. The breakout was a fifty-percent success in that Yinsen sacrificed himself to distract their captors so that the armor could be fully powered up.

Tony Stark broke free and returned to civilization, but his heart was permanently wounded and surrounded by shell fragments. Only his magnetic chest plate was able to keep the shrapnel from puncturing his heart. From that point on, Iron Man became Tony Stark's official guardian when anything arose to threaten the interests of Stark Industries, whether the threat came from spies or members of the U.S. government.

WELL-DRESSED MAN

Almost from the beginning, Iron Man began modifying his armor and he has never ceased in all his years as a super hero.

Originally the dull color of metal, the armor was quickly spray painted gold to make it more visually appealing after his date for the evening, Marion, suggested that in *Tales of Suspense #40*.

This armor served him well for a few issues until he ultimately decided that it was too unwieldy during a battle with an enemy named Mr. Doll in *Tales of Suspense #48*. At that point he substantially redesigned it into the basic format that it has today: golden leggings, arms, and faceplate, with red everywhere else.

(For a while, his faceplate had a nose on it. Why? Because one day Stan Lee happened to look at some art pages and asked, "Where's his nose?" What he meant was that the helmet seemed drawn too tightly, not allowing space for Tony's nose to fit in. Misunderstanding, the artists were warned that Lee wanted a nose on Iron Man's face.

ABOVE: The red and gold suit, familiar to modern fans, first appeared in *Tales of Suspense #48*. Art by Jack Kirby.

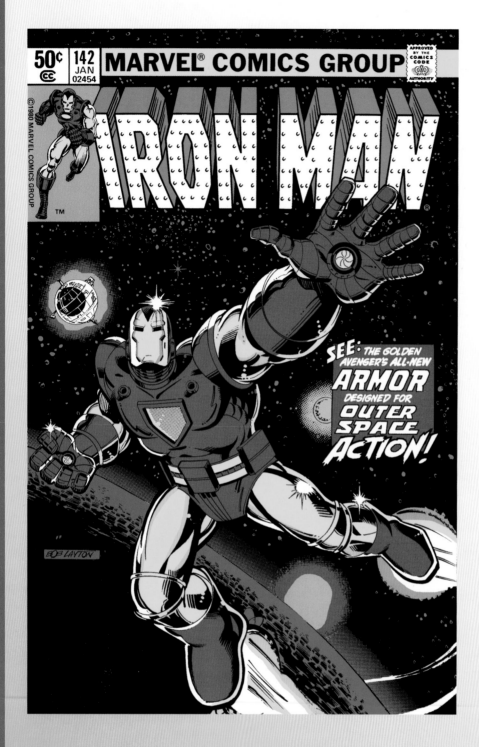

His armor has had a variety of weaponry, but there are three devices that are fairly standard. He has jet boots that enable him to fly, a unibeam in his chest that has served as a source of various light-based attacks, and, most notably, repulsor rays in his gauntlets. The source of the repulsor's power has changed in description over the years, but the bottom line is that if he hits you with repulsor rays, you'll wind up in the next county.

Some of his revisions have been specifically tailored to individual missions. Let's look at a few especially memorable ones.

Lo and behold, it was then drawn in and stayed there until Lee noticed it and asked what the heck that little triangle was doing on the front of his helmeted face.

SPACE ARMOR MK1

First appearing in *Iron Man #142,* the space armor was developed to be used in

ABOVE: Tony's deep space armor made its debut in *Iron Man #142*. Art by Bob Layton.

battle against the Sunturion, the guardian of an orbiting platform called the Well. Designed to be a source of energy, it emitted microwaves that killed the entire population of Allentown, Iowa, instead. In normal gravity, the armor is extremely awkward, but in space it's quite formidable.

STEALTH ARMOR

There have been several different versions of the stealth armor. Solid black from head to toe and first employed in *Iron Man #152*, the stealth armor was designed primarily to avoid being seen. Consequently it was much more lightweight and fragile than most other armors, and had no weapons systems. It also could distort incoming radar or sonar to help cloak its presence.

The second model of the stealth armor showed up in *Iron Man #229.* Used by Stark to penetrate Soviet airspace, the revised armor packed low-powered versions of the unibeam and repulsor rays.

HYDRO ARMOR

All of Iron Man's armor can function under water, but the hydro armor appeared in *Iron Man #218* and was designed to be able to perform at up to three miles below sea level. Stark took some cues for the weaponry from sea creatures: an electrical field like an eel's

ABOVE: The hydro armor is introduced in the pages of *Iron Man #218*. Art by Bob Layton.

ABOVE: The War Machine makes its debut in *Iron Man #281*. Art by Kevin Hopgood.

 THE AVENGERS VAULT

and the ability to generate black inky clouds like an octopus. Life-support systems were also customized for underwater survival.

ARCTIC ARMOR

This suit was employed by Tony to access his secret Arctic bunker in *Iron Man #318*. Surprisingly, the fortress did not require a giant key to open it as other super heroes' Arctic bunkers did.

HEAVY DUTY ARMOR MK1

Ever been in a situation where you know you're going to find yourself battling more than a dozen superhuman foes at one time? Then we strongly suggest that you sport something that was originally designed to slug it out with the Hulk. The Heavy Duty Armor comes equipped with serious firepower that includes several miniguns, a laser, and a force field.

WAR MACHINE

More than any other suit of armor, the War Machine, which made its first appearance in *Iron Man #281*, has developed a life of its own.

Tony crafted the War Machine after he got his head handed to him by a group of high-tech ninjas called the Masters of Silence. More heavily shielded than typical Iron Man armor, it was also tricked out with an astounding assortment of weapons including repulsors, twin chain guns, a laser blade, a wrist-mounted flamethrower, shoulder-mounted Gatling guns, a box rocket launcher, a pulse cannon, a plasma cannon, and depleted uranium.

Stark's pilot, James Rhodes, eventually wound up taking over both the armor and the identity of War Machine, functioning as a valued ally for Stark on many occasions. Eventually "Rhodey" ended up assuming a new persona: the Iron Patriot, an identity created by Norman Osborn during an invasion by Skrulls.

COURTESY OF MR. STARK

"Take that [armor] off, what are you?"
"A genius billionaire playboy philanthropist."
—Steve Rogers and Tony Stark trading words in *The Avengers*

If you're starting up a super hero team, there are few people more handy to have on it than a genius billionaire playboy philanthropist.

Over the years, the Avengers have benefited tremendously from Stark's generosity. Initially the cover story was that since Stark's personal guardian, Iron Man, was a member of the team, he had an unusual amount of pull with the boss and was thus able to acquire whatever the team needed to function, including the following:

HEADQUARTERS

The Justice League may have initially hung out in a cave, but the Avengers were way more high-tech. Their initial domicile was Avengers Mansion. Built on Fifth Avenue in 1932 as Howard Stark's townhouse, it was donated to the Avengers by the Maria Stark Foundation to use as their headquarters.

ABOVE: A view of Stark Towers as seen in *Avengers Assemble*.

 THE AVENGERS VAULT

Eventually the United Nations granted the Avengers status as a sovereign nation and the mansion was known as Avengers Embassy. Tony later sold it to Luke Cage, who used it as the headquarters for the New Avengers.

So where did the Avengers relocate to? Why, Stark Tower, a huge office structure at 58th and Broadway. Initially Tony was having trouble getting any tenants because they feared—not unreasonably—that super villains might target it for attack. So Tony donated the top three stories to the Avengers to use as their new HQ. It was destroyed several times since then (thereby lending credibility to the people who didn't want to stay there) but has since been rebuilt.

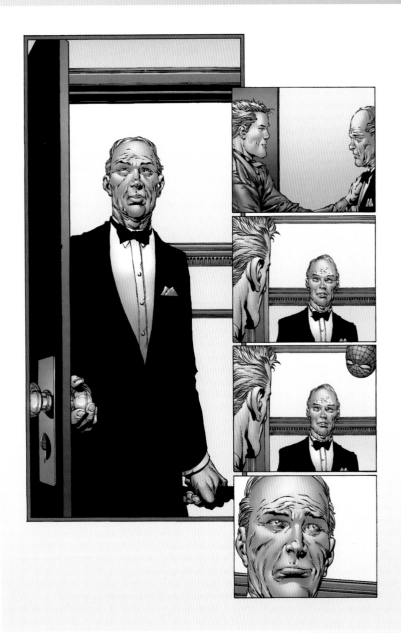

EDWIN JARVIS

Those who are only familiar with Iron Man through the movies may be surprised to discover that Jarvis is not simply a computer system, but instead an actual flesh-and-blood man.

Born and raised in Brooklyn, Jarvis served as butler to Howard and Maria Stark, and stayed on to serve Tony. When the mansion was sold, he remained with it on staff—

ABOVE: Jarvis, the Avengers' dedicated butler, from *New Avengers #3*. Art by David Finch, Danny Miki, and Frank D'Armata.

THE IRON SPIDER

Tony has always been quick to pitch in when his fellow Avengers have need of his services. One of his most conspicuous contributions was the creation of the Iron Spider costume that Peter Parker (a.k.a. Spider-Man) sported during his tenure on the Avengers. During the events of the Marvel Civil War, Peter chose to side with Tony and come out against the heroes who were resisting the Super Hero Registration Act. In doing so, Spidey revealed his secret identity. The Iron Spider costume gave Tony's now more-vulnerable teammate extra protection.

In addition to having plenty of onboard protection and the ability to glide via web mesh on the arms, the costume was most notable for the three waldoes (mechanical arms) on its back that extended into full-sized spider arms. They could see around walls via cameras in the tips, and also pick up objects.

in fact, he's pretty much the only staff—and served the Avengers in every possible capacity, ranging from preparing meals to keeping their vehicles in top shape. Over the fifty years of their existence, he has been one of the few constants in the organization, always there to lend a hand or provide whatever services are required.

ABOVE: Tony Stark isn't the only Marvel character wearing armor. Here's Peter Parker in his Stark-created Iron Spider armor.

THE AVENGERS VAULT

Peter was happy to employ the armor until he eventually soured on the notion that he was functioning against other super heroes. His subsequent discovery that Tony was using the armor to keep an eye on his whereabouts caused him to dump it soon after. Tony then turned the armor over to a new team, the Scarlet Spiders, who used it to battle various super villains.

WORKING BEHIND THE SCENES

Although there are few people in the Marvel Universe who have so thoroughly embraced being in the public eye, Tony never stopped operating behind the scenes as well.

At some point, with all the alien races that seemed to have set their sights on Earth, Tony decided that certain people possessed information that could be put to concrete preventative use. As a result, he formed a secretive group called the Illuminati, composed of Black Bolt, the Black Panther, Professor X, Reed Richards, Prince Namor, and Doctor Strange. The group then proceeded to get involved in a variety of cosmic-level endeavors, ranging

ABOVE: What happens when the smartest guys in the Marvel Universe form their own club? You get *The New Avengers: Illuminati #1*. Art by Jim Cheung and Justin Ponsor.

YOU'VE GOTTA HAVE HEART

ABOVE: Tony faces his alcoholism in the classic *Iron Man #128*. Art by Bob Layton.

from confronting the Skrulls and warning them never to attack Earth again, to hiding the various gems of the Infinity Gauntlet to make sure that it was never used again.

The Illuminati's biggest mistake was probably their endeavor to rid the world of the Hulk by shooting him into space. That went great—right up until the Hulk found his way back to Earth months later and declared World War Hulk upon the Illuminati, systematically defeating each of them and eventually forcing them to battle in an arena. They managed to defeat him—but barely.

The Illuminati were central participants during the Skrulls' Secret Invasion of Earth, and by the end of it were so fed up that the group split. Eventually, however, they reconvened.

HIS ARMOR CAN PROTECT HIM AGAINST ANYTHING, EXCEPT HIMSELF

I came up with that line.

Back in my days as Marvel Direct Sales Manager, editor/writer Denny O'Neil came to my office greatly excited. Writer of the *Iron Man* title at the time, Denny was planning to reopen a story line first written by David Michelinie in *Iron Man #120–#128*. Entitled "Demon in a Bottle!," the story explored Tony Stark's excessive drinking and eventually had him come to terms with the fact that he was an alcoholic. It was Denny's idea to have him fall off the wagon and he wanted me involved in promoting it. I immediately came up with that promotional line and Denny declared, "I love that! That's great!" Which was what we used to push the series when it launched.

We must have done something right, because the subsequent story line proved so popular that certain aspects of it—including the introduction of Obadiah Stane and creation of the Iron Monger—wound up being used in the first Iron Man film. Since that time, alcoholism has continued to inform Tony's actions and has always been a continuing menace for his character, bubbling just below the surface.

A TROUBLED AVENGER

As much of a problem as alcoholism has been to Tony Stark, he has also had his share of other difficulties. Indeed, some of his troubles and actions have polarized fan opinion toward him from time to time. Some of these endeavors have included:

BEING EXPELLED FROM THE AVENGERS

For a time Tony found himself going head-to-head with an industrial rival named Justin Hammer, who had found a way to steal Tony's armor. During what became known as the Armor Wars, Tony accidentally killed the second Titanium Man. This, along with other vigilante actions, prompted the U.S. government to declare Iron Man an outlaw. The Avengers likewise turned against him and banished him from the team. At the time, people didn't realize that Tony Stark and Iron Man were one and the same, and Tony took the step of publicly siding against Iron Man and declaring that he had fired him from his employ. He then resumed his activities as Iron Man in new armor while telling the world that the guy in the previous armor had died and he was someone completely new.

CIVIL WAR

One of the most fractious events in the history of the Marvel Universe, the civil war resulted after a group of young heroes, the New Warriors, fought a battle that ended in the deaths of hundreds, including children, in Stamford, Connecticut. During the public outrage that followed, Tony stepped forward and suggested the creation of a Super Hero Registration Act. Every person operating as a super hero would have to reveal his or her identity to the government, and the ones with less experience would have to submit to training. Tony's own bouts with alcoholism left him quite aware of what someone could do with superpowers if they weren't fully in control of them.

But the Act saw major blowback when a number of heroes, including Captain America, strenuously objected to the new law. This resulted in all-out battles between the two groups of heroes until Captain America eventually surrendered in order to avoid any more collateral damage. When Cap was subsequently gunned down by a sniper, Tony felt incredibly guilty over what the Registration Act had led to.

When Norman Osborn rose to power, Tony took extraordinary steps to make sure that Osborn would be unable to discover the secret identities of his fellow heroes. Tony eventually wound up in a mentally vegetative state, but he pulled out of it with help from his friends.

And that's just a sample of the things that Tony Stark has had to endure, with life

WHOSE SIDE...
...ARE YOU ON?

THE MARVEL UNIVERSE IS CHANGING. IN THE WAKE OF A TRAGEDY, CAPITOL HILL PROPOSES THE SUPER HERO REGISTRATION ACT, REQUIRING ALL COSTUMED HEROES TO UNMASK THEMSELVES BEFORE THE GOVERNMENT. DIVIDED, THE NATION'S GREATEST CHAMPIONS MUST EACH DECIDE HOW TO REACT—A DECISION THAT WILL ALTER THE COURSE OF THEIR LIVES FOREVER!

MARK MILLAR

STEVE MCNIVEN

DEXTER VINES

MORRY HOLLOWELL

CIVIL WAR

A MARVEL COMICS EVENT IN SEVEN PARTS

MARVEL

1

experiences ranging from rock bottom to, for a time, leading S.H.I.E.L.D. Yet his most reliable attribute is his ability to eventually bounce back from whatever he's faced.

BAD GUYS, PART THREE

There's an old saying that a hero is judged by the enemies he makes, and Tony has made some formidable ones in his career. Some of them have been armored, while others have

wielded unique weapons arrays, proving more than a challenge for him.

THE MANDARIN

Hands down the most famous and relentless of Iron Man's enemies, the Mandarin is a direct descendant of Genghis Khan. He was raised to detest society and seek ways to bring it down. His first and greatest weapon in that endeavor was his discovery

ABOVE: The creation of a law demanding that all super heroes register their identities with S.H.I.E.L.D. results in a civil war pitting hero against hero. Art by Steve McNiven and Morry Hollowell.

of the remains of a fallen alien in the Valley of Spirits. The alien possessed ten rings of formidable power. The Mandarin took those rings and launched a war on civilization.

He first showed up in *Tales of Suspense #50* and has spent decades doing battle with Iron Man. Tony Stark initially confronted the Mandarin when he was sent by the U.S. government to check him out, and was almost defeated before managing to escape. Since then they have repeatedly fought each other, and the Mandarin has seemingly died any number of times but keeps managing to find a way back. He found time to sire a son, Temujin, whom he sent to live in a monastery.

CRIMSON DYNAMO

First appearing in *Tales of Suspense #46*, the Crimson Dynamo was a suit of armor created by Russian scientist Anton Vanko. Vanko was then sent on a mission to destroy Tony Stark's bodyguard. But Iron Man tricked Vanko into believing that his own government was planning to dispose of him, and he wound up switching sides and becoming a valued employee of Stark Industries. Eventually the government sent two agents—Boris Turgenev and the Black Widow—to retrieve Vanko, and Turgenev stole the armor. Vanko wound up killing Boris, but died in the process.

Since then, eight different people have gone by the name of Crimson Dynamo. A couple of them have been parts of groups (the Titanic Three, the Supreme Soviets)

ABOVE: The Mandarin, in his first appearance in *Tales of Suspense #50*. Art by Jack Kirby and George Roussos.

ENCLOSED 1: "All About Iron Man" special featurette from *Tales of Suspense #55*. Art by Don Heck.

ENCLOSED 2: Jack Kirby's original art from *Avenger's #1* showing Iron Man intercepting Loki's decoy distress call.

Soviets came up with another armor-clad operative. The Titanium Man debuted in *Tales of Suspense #69*. KGB member Boris Bullski came up with the notion of winning a propaganda war against the United States by defeating Iron Man in combat. To this end, he used the departed Professor Vanko's laboratory to develop a new and formidable armor that was twice the size of Iron Man's. He challenged Iron Man to a battle, televised worldwide, and Iron Man accepted. Naturally Tony beat the crap out of him.

Titanium Man reappeared repeatedly throughout Iron Man's career, and Tony Stark even hired Bullski once to fake an attack on Congress in order to convince them to repeal the Super Hero Registration Act.

Various other individuals have shown up as Titanium Man from time to time, including a Kree captain who had been dispatched to steal Iron Man's armor.

and pretty much all of them have endeavored to make Iron Man's life difficult.

TITANIUM MAN

Dissatisfied with the way the whole Crimson Dynamo business turned out, the

ABOVE: The Crimson Dynamo first showed up to harass Iron Man in the pages of *Tales of Suspense #46*. Art by Jack Kirby and Dick Ayers.

THE AVENGERS VAULT

BLACK WIDOW AND HAWKEYE

Yes, we know that they're both super heroes and members of the Avengers. But it's worth noting that wasn't always the case.

When Natasha Romanova (originally Romanoff until artist/writer Frank Miller pointed out that, being a woman, she should have feminized her last name) first showed up in *Tales of Suspense #52*, she was a Soviet spy and one of Tony Stark's most formidable opponents. Rescued as a child from certain death in a burning building by a Soviet soldier named Ivan (who became her lifelong companion), Natasha attracted the attention of Soviet intelligence and began her training at a young age.

Initially she romanced Tony Stark to acquire an antigravity ray, but when her cover was blown, she turned her attentions to one Clint Barton, a.k.a. Hawkeye.

Clint Barton, orphaned at a young age, was raised in a circus where he learned the art of archery from the Swordsman—with whom he had a falling out after discovering that the Swordsman was stealing money from the carnival.

Eventually he went out on his own and one day witnessed Iron Man saving some people's lives. This prompted him to decide that he too wanted to become a super hero, so he crafted himself a costume and came up with the identity of Hawkeye. Unfortunately on his first outing the police mistook him for a criminal, and he found himself on the wrong side of the law.

ABOVE: Long before he was a good guy, Hawkeye the Archer was an opponent of Iron Man's, debuting in *Tales of Suspense #57*. Art by Don Heck.

YOU'VE GOTTA HAVE HEART

masters and ended up dividing her time between S.H.I.E.L.D. and the Avengers.

WHIPLASH

Iron Man has had to fight various evil organizations, including AIM (Advanced Idea Mechanics), Hydra, and the Maggia. Whiplash was a Maggia employee. Mark Scarlotti, a brilliant electrical technician, decided that he was more suited to be a criminal. So he devised a formidable metal whip and, on the Maggia's behalf, attacked Iron Man back in *Tales of Suspense #97*. He was defeated.

Years later—in 1981, to be specific—he changed his name to Backlash and under the employ of Justin Hammer once again took on Iron Man. The same result ensued.

Shortly thereafter he met the Black Widow, and she seduced him into helping her go up against Iron Man. Before too long, though, Hawkeye wound up regretting his decision and joined the Avengers.

Eventually he managed to convince the Black Widow to join him on the right side of the law. She rebelled against her Soviet

Eventually Scarlotti decided to walk away from his criminal life. He married and had a child, but his wife was killed and so he was dragged back into the underworld. Eventually he faced off against Iron Man and actually had him on the ropes, but Iron Man's armor—which

ABOVE: The comic-book version of Anton Vanko as Whiplash made his debut in *Iron Man vs. Whiplash #1*. Art by Phillipe Briones and Matt Milla.

had gained sentience—killed him against Tony's wishes.

The next Whiplash was one Anton Vanko, amazingly of no relation to the Anton Vanko who became the Crimson Dynamo. This time around, Vanko was a young scientist whose small home-town was obliterated by someone wearing Iron Man armor in order to frame Tony Stark. The trick worked and Vanko created the Whiplash armor to hunt him down. Eventually he found out that Stark was indeed framed, but that didn't turn him away from his villainous pursuits.

COOL EXEC WITH A HEART OF STEEL

Tony Stark's involvement with the Avengers was both the best and worst thing that could have happened to the team.

As quite possibly one of the wealthiest men in the Marvel Universe, Stark enabled the team to function as a group with both a headquarters and the unending support of Stark resources.

On the other hand, his personal failings and support of the Super Hero Registration Act severely splintered the team, resulting

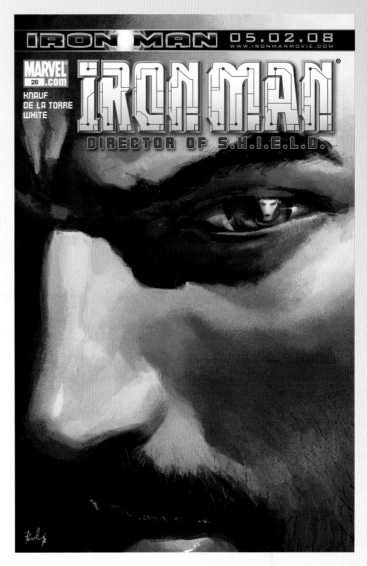

in multiple Avengers groups all functioning in opposition to each other.

In the final analysis, we have to take the highs with the lows. Tony rests in Marvel's upper echelons so when he falls it's going to be much farther and deeper than most. And the fans have proven that they're more than willing to stick with him for the ride.

ABOVE: The cover of *Iron Man: Director of S.H.I.E.L.D. #28.* Art by Gerald Panel.

5

"DOC BRUCE BANNER,
BELTED BY GAMMA RAYS, TURNS INTO THE
HULK . . ."

IN AN INTERVIEW WITH *THE COMICS JOURNAL,* JACK

Kirby explained how he came up with the incredible Hulk: "I created [him] when I saw a woman lift a car. Her baby was caught under the running board of this car. . . . It suddenly came to me that in desperation we can all do that—we can knock down walls, we can go berserk, which we do. You know what happens when [you're] in a rage—you can tear a house down."

This is an interesting recollection, considering that the Hulk's origins had, in fact, nothing to do with strength generated by rage. Apparently Kirby was remembering something that happened in the 1978 *Incredible Hulk* television pilot episode, in which a woman recounts lifting a car to free her son.

OPPOSITE: The Incredible Hulk, ready to smash.

scientist Robert Bruce Banner (the "Robert" courtesy of a later memory slip in *The Avengers #4* when Lee had him say, "I've changed back to Bob Banner!"), and by night, a ton of raging gray strength that some soldiers wound up nicknaming the Hulk. By the next issue he was green, and that was the color he stayed for decades. It's understandable that the Hulk's true origins would slip Kirby's mind: within the first six issues his entire process for transforming would change to the point where Bruce was willingly stepping in front of an oversized gamma ray blaster device in order to trigger the transformation.

Even Stan Lee didn't recall it. When reminded of the Hulk's origins, he said in surprise, "I wonder why we changed it?!"

To the best of Lee's recollection, the Hulk's origins came from the classic *Frankenstein*.

"Truth is—I always loved Boris Karloff's old Frankenstein movie," he said. "Far as I can remember, the monster didn't want to

The rage aspect wasn't established until two years after the Hulk's comic debut, and Dick Ayers penciled that issue of *Tales to Astonish #59*.

In the first issue of the Hulk's own title, which appeared in May 1962, the Hulk's transformation was actually locked into a day/night cycle. By day, he was puny

ABOVE: In *Tales to Astonish #59,* Giant Man travels to New Mexico to convince the Hulk to rejoin the team. Things don't go as planned. Art by Dick Ayers and Paul Reinman.

 THE AVENGERS VAULT

ABOVE: Cover of *The Incredible Hulk #1,* featuring a gray Hulk. Art by Jack Kirby.

"DOC BRUCE BANNER, BELTED BY GAMMA RAYS, TURNS INTO THE HULK..."

hurt anyone, but those idiots with torches were always chasing him up and down the mountain. To me, the monster was the good guy.

"One day it occurred to me it might be fun to do a monstrous type of hero who really was a good guy but, because of the way he looked, everyone was always hounding him and trying to destroy him. Then I felt it might be fun to use the Dr. Jekyll and Mr. Hyde angle. The monster was really a normal man, a good man, who turned into the monster. I decided rage would be a good reason for the man-to-monster transformation.

"Naturally, the easiest way to do it was to make him a scientist who was hit by gamma rays while saving a teenager's life (thus showing the reader what a good guy he was). Of course, he wouldn't want anyone to know that he was the monster who the law was always trying to catch—and who the bad guys were always trying to kill."

THIS IS ONLY A TEST

If we're going to stick to strict common sense, the Hulk's origin really doesn't hold together.

In a New Mexico army base, scientist Bruce Banner is preparing to test his new weapon, the gamma bomb. His assistant is a scientist named Igor who turns out to be a Russian spy. So when the bomb is counting down to detonation and Bruce suddenly sees that a teenager has wandered onto the site, he orders Igor to halt the countdown while Banner goes out to clear the kid away. Igor naturally does nothing to prevent the bomb from detonating, but Bruce is able to push the kid—teenager Rick Jones—to safety, getting hammered by the detonating gamma rays himself.

This, of course, doesn't make a lick of sense. There were soldiers all around. Bruce should have halted the countdown himself and had the soldiers remove the teenager. Why did he feel the need to take any sort of risk and go after the straying teenager?

Go figure.

In any event, the gamma blast permeated Banner's molecular structure, and when nighttime fell, for some reason, Bruce Banner transformed into a mass of gray muscle dubbed the Hulk. From a production point of view, gray proved too difficult a skin color to be maintained consistently, and by issue #2 he was green. The gray

ABOVE: The moment that started it all in *The Incredible Hulk #1*: Doc Bruce Banner is belted by gamma rays after saving teenage intruder Rick Jones. Art by Jack Kirby and Paul Reinman.

"DOC BRUCE BANNER, BELTED BY GAMMA RAYS, TURNS INTO THE HULK..."

worked into the series continuity and writer Al Milgrom even brought the gray Hulk directly into the series for a time.

SO WHAT'S HIS DEAL?

In the interests of full disclosure I should mention that I wrote the Hulk for twelve years starting in the 1990s. One of the major things I was criticized for was messing with the original concept of the Hulk since during much of my run he was gray. (I chose to maintain Al Milgrom's transformation.) The Hulk was also perfectly articulate, having a full command of personal pronouns that the more familiar "Hulk smash" incarnation never possessed.

coloration was addressed in later reprints that depicted him as green from the get-go, but eventually his early gray shading was

ABOVE: Hulk leaps into the air in *Incredible Hulk #3*. Art by Jack Kirby and Dick Ayers.

I always found that criticism amusing, considering I was in fact portraying the Hulk truer to his roots than most who came after me.

The fact is that the Hulk went through so many incarnations in his first six issues that virtually any portrayal of the Hulk is going to be consistent with his origins.

In the first two issues, the Hulk was depicted as perfectly articulate. He was terse, certainly, but he referred to himself in the first person. And, as mentioned, his transformations were day/night.

By issue #3, he wound up being exposed to cosmic rays, which made him not only mute but capable of being the Hulk in the daytime.

As of issue #4, Bruce was now controlling the transformations with the gamma machine and also possessed his own mind as the Hulk, or at least a more brutish form of his intelligence. When he was Bruce he talked in his formal, scientific manner, but as the Hulk, he bore more of a resemblance to the Thing—whose popularity among fans had also factored into the creation of the Hulk in the first place.

And that was how the Hulk's personality was shaped through to issue #6, when his solo title was unceremoniously

ABOVE: Bruce attempts experiments that will give him control over his transformations in *Incredible Hulk #4*. The endeavor works, for a little while. Art by Jack Kirby and Dick Ayers.

"DOC BRUCE BANNER, BELTED BY GAMMA RAYS, TURNS INTO THE HULK..."

canceled. He bounced around in the pages of *The Avengers* and *The Fantastic Four* for a brief time before landing in his own series in *Tales to Astonish*.

SOME ASSEMBLY REQUIRED

It's somehow poetic that the very first opponent the Avengers faced was the Hulk.

Loki, their true foe, manipulated events so that it seemed as if the Hulk had gone on a rampage. By the end of the issue, the Hulk, who was making his first appearance since his own title had been canceled, agreed to join the team for the simplest reason of all: it was better to be with them than against them.

This resolve lasted exactly one issue. During their confrontation with the Space Phantom in issue #2, the Phantom took the form of the Hulk and performed all manner of mischief. This prompted the Avengers to say many nasty things about the Hulk, which he, rather unsurprisingly, took to heart. By the end of the issue he had broken off from the team entirely, and by issue #3 he had joined forces with Sub-Mariner to battle his former associates.

Ironically, Rick Jones was heavily involved with the team's creation. The team wound up coming together because Rick, upon hearing of the Hulk's supposed destruction of a train trestle, radioed the Fantastic Four for help. Loki, whose Asgardian heritage apparently included a doctorate in electronics, managed to reroute the broadcast so that Thor would hear it. However, Iron Man and Ant-Man also heard it, so they got in on the action as well. Yet when the Hulk left the Avengers, Rick sort of hung around, and one thing led to another until . . .

DUDE, WHERE'S MY SIDEKICK?

It is entirely possible to say that no Avengers' supporting cast has gone through more changes than the Hulk's.

When the series began, there were three main supporting players: Rick Jones, Thaddeus "Thunderbolt" Ross, and Ross's daughter Betty.

Rick has gone through a series of permutations, most recently being transformed into a gamma-irradiated individual named the A-Bomb. Thunderbolt, the belligerent general who oversaw the development of the gamma bomb and despised the weakling Banner, spent much of his time pursuing the Hulk, and was himself changed into the red-skinned Red Hulk.

ABOVE: In the pages of *Avengers #2*, Rick Jones discovers the Space Phantom has taken the Hulk's place. Art by Jack Kirby, Paul Reinman, and Stan Goldberg.

"DOC BRUCE BANNER, BELTED BY GAMMA RAYS, TURNS INTO THE HULK..."

ABOVE: In *Captain America #110,* Rick Jones returns to take Bucky Barnes's place alongside Captain America, setting off the Hulk's jealous rage. Art by Jim Steranko.

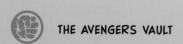

MOST DESIRABLE

Rick Jones has a lengthy history in the Marvel Universe, and initially his role was "most desirable sidekick."

When Jones first met Captain America, the good captain was quite startled, mistaking Rick for his own deceased sidekick, Bucky Barnes (who would later turn out, in best Marvel fashion, not to be deceased at all). It took Cap a little while to sort out that the lad facing him wasn't Bucky, but instead simply looked like him. Jack Kirby had drawn both and done little to distinguish the two teens.

Taking an immediate liking to the First Avenger (an ironic name considering Cap wasn't even on the team in issue #1), Rick started vying for an opportunity to become the new Bucky. Cap initially resisted the idea. He was still carrying a boatload of guilt over the initial Bucky's demise and wasn't sanguine about risking another teen's life in his adventures. As for Rick, he had guilt problems of his own, still feeling responsible for Bruce Banner's transformation into the Hulk. That guilt caused him to return to the Hulk's side for a time, but eventually in *Captain America #110* he returned to Cap and this time the Captain did indeed take

him on as a partner. Rick donned Bucky's uniform and received training from arguably the best hand-to-hand fighter in the Marvel Universe.

He eventually returned to the Hulk, then split a few more times, but there was no denying the connection between the two.

BETTY BYE

And then there's Betty.

Betty started life as a simple girl who lost her mother at a young age. She was raised at boarding schools because her father felt that military bases were no place for young ladies. When we first met her in *Incredible Hulk #1*, she was sharing longing

ABOVE: Bruce Banner dreads the eventual transformation back into the Hulk in the pages of *Incredible Hulk #1*. Art by Jack Kirby and Dick Ayers.

his time as a green-skinned monster. Eventually Bruce managed to gain control of his transformations and they were to be married. But the Hulk's archenemy, the Leader, showed up and changed Bruce back into the rampaging Hulk. This, combined with the Hulk's later involvement with a Microverse princess named Jarella, prompted Betty to forget about Bruce and instead marry Major Glenn Talbot, who had been pining after her for years.

Naturally their relationship didn't work out in the long run, and Betty wound up having a complete nervous breakdown. At this point, the evil MODOK of

stares with Bruce Banner, which only irritated her father even more.

Bruce's transformation into the Hulk provided serious problems for their relationship. Naturally Betty had no idea that her skinny boyfriend was spending half

AIM transformed her into a winged creature called the Harpy with the intention of having her kill the Hulk. This worked out about as well as you can imagine, and eventually she was transformed back to her normal self.

ABOVE: Betty is transformed into the Harpy in *Incredible Hulk #168*. Art by Herb Trimpe and Stan Goldberg.

Betty wound up divorcing Talbot and marrying Bruce Banner during a ceremony fraught with its own craziness. For a while they were separated when Betty was convinced that Bruce had died in an explosion, but eventually they were reunited and went on the run together. They lived in Florida for a time before separating once again . . .

And then things got really bad. A longtime villain of the Hulk, the Abomination (more on him shortly), decided to kill Betty by poisoning her with his own blood, leading the Hulk to temporarily believe that her condition was caused by her lengthy association with him. Betty subsequently died, or at least so Bruce believed—it turned out that her father, General Thunderbolt Ross (more on him shortly as well), had her body cryogenically frozen, doubtless feeling that if freezing the body worked for Captain America, it would work for his daughter.

He turned out to be correct. The combined talents of the Leader and MODOK not only revived Betty, but changed her yet

again, this time into a red-skinned She-Hulk. It is in that identity that she continues to romp around the Marvel Universe.

HULK AND KIDS

Twenty years ago Marvel editors thought fatherhood would diminish Hulk's appeal with fans, and a story line I wrote where Betty was pregnant ended with her losing

ABOVE: In *Incredible Hulk #319*, Bruce Banner—now separated from the Hulk—marries Betty. Art by John Byrne, Keith Williams, and Andy Yanchus.

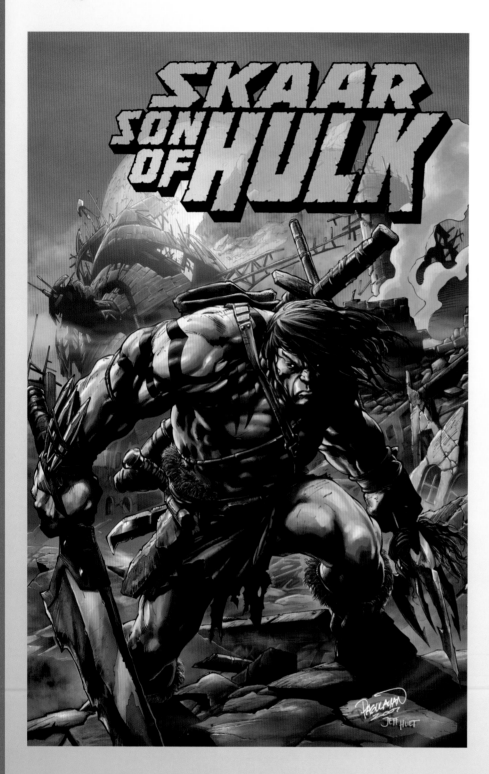

SKAAR AND HIRO-KALA

When the Illuminati thought it would be a great idea to shoot the Hulk off into space, it never occurred to them that not only would he return, but that he'd be towing a family!

The Hulk landed on the far-off planet of Sakaar, a world full of barbarian-level combat. He wound up butting heads with the evil king's bodyguard, the beautiful Caiera. Caiera was one of the few members of her race to master the Old Power—a version of the Power Cosmic—which gave her control over the Earth. She eventually switched sides, fighting alongside the Hulk and, after overthrowing the king, they married. She wound up pregnant with twins: Skaar and Hiro-Kala, the baby. Times have changed and now Hulk has more kids than any other Marvel character.

ABOVE: Skaar, the son of Hulk, was conceived during the Hulk's sojourn to the planet Sakaar. Art by Jose Ladrónn.

born from a cocoon that had fallen into the Lake of Fire.

Skaar grew from infant to teenager within the course of a year, and from that into a young man. His world was eventually consumed by Galactus, but by that point Skaar was already on his way to Earth. Once here, he resumed a somewhat fractious relationship with his father, who did his best to befriend him with limited success. Skaar eventually joined the Dark Avengers working as a spy for Captain America.

In addition to being a self-trained weapons master, Skaar also has strength that rivals his father. Plus he can transform into the human identity of a twelve-year-old boy.

Hiro-Kala didn't end up with the same set of skills as his twin. He was something of a weakling as a child. However through various adventures he grew to become a leader of his people, and when his world was destroyed by Galactus, he led them in search of a new planet on which to reside. Eventually, after a voyage to the Microverse, he set his sights on Earth with the intention of destroying it, but wound up being beaten and imprisoned in rock by the combined efforts of his father and twin brother. Although he lacked the physical strength of

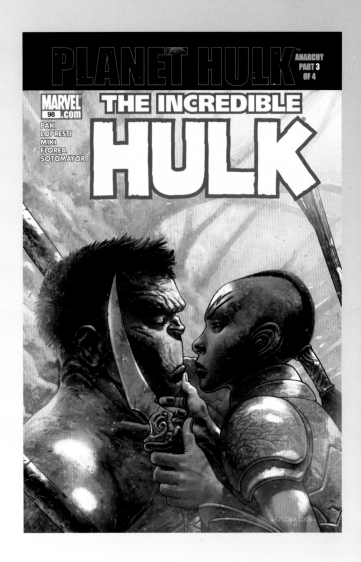

his father and brother, his mastery of the Old Power and his skills as a swordsman made him formidable.

LYRA

There are literally thousands of alternate Earths in the Marvel Universe. On 23rd Century Earth-8009, there is a valiant warrior by the name of Thundra. She was a member of the United Sisterhood Republic

ABOVE: The cover of *Incredible Hulk #98,* which features the Planet Hulk storyline. Art by Jose Ladrónn.

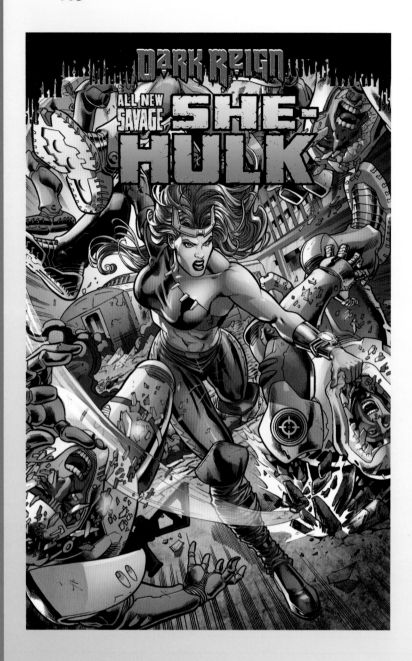

to her own time. She then extracted the Hulk's DNA from her saliva and used it to create a child: the formidable Lyra.

Possessing the strength of her parents—putting her on par with She-Hulk—Lyra has the additional wrinkle of getting weaker as she gets angrier, which forces her to keep control of herself. She found her way to modern-day Earth, where she continues to have adventures, although her lack of experience with men has made normal interaction difficult for her.

BAD GUYS, PART FOUR

If an effective bad guy is someone who serves as an opposite to the hero, then the Hulk's list of hostiles is unquestionably on target. His most consistent enemies are either the personification of intelligence or else the definition of strength—both used to bring destruction and suffering upon others.

THE LEADER

(the new name for what was formerly the United States), and perpetually harassed by the men of the time. The Sisterhood decided they needed some additional power on their side. So Thundra came to Earth-616, tracked down the Hulk, battled him for a bit, and then kissed him before returning

Sam Sterns was an ordinary guy working in a janitorial position at a chemical plant when

---

ABOVE: Hulk's daughter, Lyra, had her own title briefly. Art by Peter Vale and Marte Gracia.

he wound up being accidentally bombarded by gamma radiation during an explosion of radioactive materials. Not only did he turn green, but his brain insanely expanded (straight up, for some reason), giving him hyperintelligent abilities. From there, he kicked off his criminal career as the Leader, during which he would—through a variety of means—try to find ways to take over the Earth and live up to his new name.

Time and again he would go head-to-head with the Hulk, and to his great frustration his incredible intellect did him no good against the pure strength of his adversary.

He was killed several times, in several ways, from falling into a volcano to being eaten by a polar bear. But somehow he's always managed to find his way back to life so that he can continue to harass the Hulk.

THE ABOMINATION

Emil Blonsky began life in much the same way as many typical Marvel villains: as a Soviet spy. Unlike the accidental exposure to gamma rays that inflicted both Banner and Sterns, Blonsky deliberately exposed himself to a far greater dosage of radiation than the Hulk sustained. The result was that he became a massive, scaled super villain so powerful that in his first time out of the box, he actually defeated the Hulk. They went on to clash many times over the years.

The Abomination's motives have shifted often. Starting out as a purely villainous

ABOVE: Tales to Astonish #63 reveals the origin of the Leader, the Hulk's most persistent enemy. Art by Steve Ditko and George Bell.

"DOC BRUCE BANNER, BELTED BY GAMMA RAYS, TURNS INTO THE HULK..."

brute, he eventually morphed into a sympathetic character living in New York's sewers. But when his wife, Nadia, fled him because of his physical transformation, he wound up blaming Banner for her departure and decided to get back at him by poisoning Banner's wife, Betty. This ultimately led to a confrontation with the Red Hulk, namely Betty's father, who wound up gunning down the Abomination. Since then he's been hanging out with various death gods, but there's little doubt he'll be back.

THUNDERBOLT ROSS

Thunderbolt Ross, more than anyone, pursued and challenged the Hulk year in, year out. Ross had nothing but contempt for Bruce Banner's romantic intentions toward his daughter Betty. He spent countless hours and doubtless millions of dollars in

ABOVE: The Red Hulk was revealed to be Thunderbolt Ross in *Hulk Vol. 2, #23*. Art by Ed McGuinness.

ENCLOSED 1: This 1976 original illustration of the Hulk was the last piece of published art Jack Kirby drew for Marvel Comics.

ENCLOSED 2: Original interior pencil art by Leinil Yu for pages 12–13 of *Indestructible Hulk #1*.

military hardware trying to capture or kill the Hulk, but he always fell short.

Many years later, Ross faked his own death with the help of a life model decoy and, through the aid of the Super-Soldier program, wound up transforming himself into a red-skinned Hulk. His identity was hidden for some time, but after initially beating up an assortment of Marvel heroes, the Red Hulk was drafted into the Avengers and is currently leading the Thunderbolts.

THE U-FOES

Some people will go to great lengths to emulate their heroes. In this case, millionaire Simon Utrecht thought it would be a good idea to imitate the way the Fantastic Four acquired their powers. So in *Incredible Hulk #254*, he assembled a flight team consisting of Ann and Jimmy Darnell and Mike Steel, and they launched themselves into space. What they didn't know is that they were on track to overdose on cosmic rays and die, except that Bruce Banner, who happened to be in the area at the time, reprogrammed their computers and brought them down before the exposure reached terminal levels.

So naturally they hated him for interfering and became his sworn enemies. They did indeed gain superpowers and new identities. Simon became Vector, a telekinetic who could repel or attract matter. Ann was Vapor, capable of transforming her body into various gases, including poisonous ones. Her kid brother, Jimmy, became X-Ray, a living energy field who could unleash radioactive blasts. And Mike Steel became the appropriately named Iron Clad, whose body was made of transformed metal.

THE MAESTRO

A hundred years from now, long after wars have reduced humanity to a limited few, the main city that still exists is called Dystopia. Dystopia is ruled by the formidable Maestro who is, in fact, a future version of the Hulk. He is, however, even stronger than the Hulk because he's spent an additional hundred years absorbing free-floating radiation left over from various wars.

Balding with a white beard, the Maestro reigns supreme over the residents of the land until a handful of rebels finds Doctor Doom's time machine and uses it to bring forward the one individual who might be able to take down the Maestro: the modern-day Hulk. The Hulk embarks on an epic battle that ends with him transporting

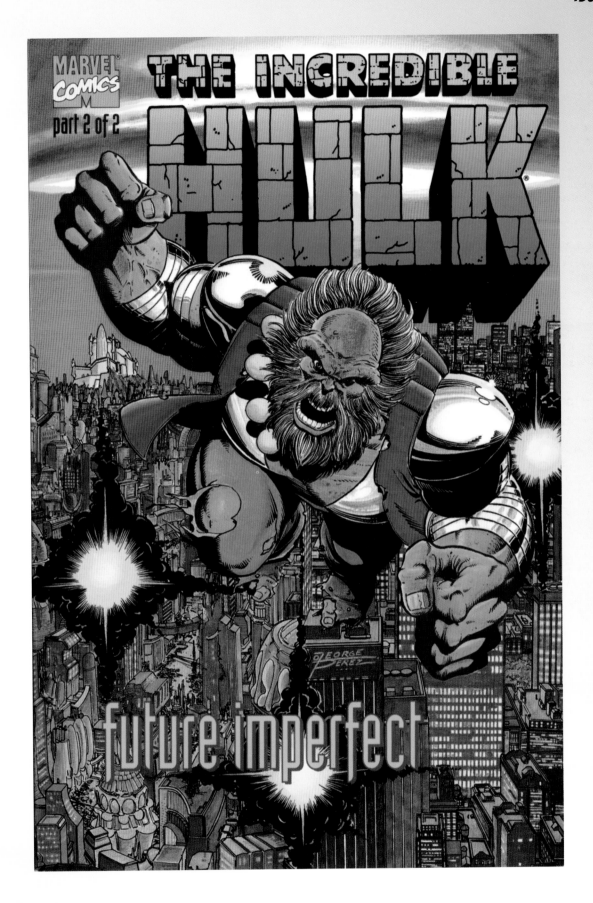

ABOVE: The Hulk goes head-to-head against himself in the two-part *Future Imperfect,* drawn by George Perez.

"DOC BRUCE BANNER, BELTED BY GAMMA RAYS, TURNS INTO THE HULK..."

Avengers. On various occasions he has fought head-to-head with Thor, Iron Man, and Captain America. Each battle has ended inconclusively, but one always got the impression that if the fights had continued ad infinitum, eventually the Hulk would win. It would seem inevitable, because whoever he's fighting, sooner or later, has to run out of strength. The Hulk, on the other hand, never gets tired. Instead, the angrier he gets, the stronger he gets, and that strength never stops coming.

Indeed, it's hard to think of anyone in the Marvel Universe that the Hulk has not fought at some point or other. And whenever those battles have occurred, the various Marvel heroes have often tried everything they can think of to find a way to back out of it. The simple reality is this: no one really wants to face off against the Hulk because they know that, at most, they will manage to survive. No one actually believes they're going to be able to defeat the Hulk.

the Maestro back to ground zero of the gamma bomb, a blast even the Maestro cannot survive. So the Hulk effectively begins and ends at the same moment.

MY ENEMY, MY ALLY

The Hulk has had, to put it mildly, the most fractious relationship with his fellow

ABOVE: Iron Man's Hulkbuster armor appeared in *World War Hulk #1*. Art by John Romita, Jr., Klaus Janson, and Christina Strain.

 THE AVENGERS VAULT

ABOVE: Cover art for *Avengers vs. Atlas #3,* by Gabriel Hardman and Betty Breitweiser.

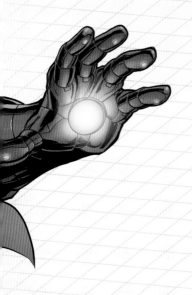

6

BEYOND THE
UNIVERSE

THE AVENGERS' ADVENTURES HAVE HARDLY BEEN
limited to the comics, or even to their epic silver-screen debut
in 2012. In point of fact, the Avengers were gracing television
screens within a few years of their creation, and have continued ever since.

THE MARVEL SUPER HEROES

The Marvel Super Heroes was Marvel's first foray into television,
and for all its mechanical limitations, it could not have been
more faithful to its origins. Indeed, it is probably more devoted
to the source material than any adaptation in Marvel history.

The Marvel Super Heroes consisted of sixty-five episodes
that were direct adaptations of previously printed stories.
And by direct, we mean panel-by-panel. Each seven-minute

OPPOSITE: The Avengers: Earth's Mightiest Heroes.

segment had dialogue pulled from word balloons and artwork directly lifted from the comics pages. So directly, in fact, that the cartoon scarcely moved. The characters' lips moved, semi-timed with the words, and on occasion we'd see Thor swing his hammer or Cap hurl his shield.

Produced by Grantray-Lawrence Animation, *The Marvel Super Heroes* wasn't an Avengers cartoon per se, but it featured four of the earliest members. It ran five days a week, with Captain America on Monday, the Hulk on Tuesday, Iron Man on Wednesday, and Thor on Thursday (of course). Friday was given over to the Sub-Mariner who wasn't an Avenger, but fought them in issue #3, so that's not bad. Furthermore, *Avengers #2* was actually adapted in the Hulk's cartoon.

The cartoons were produced via a process called Xerography, which involved photocopying the comic-book pages. Animators didn't especially worry about frame-to-frame continuity. For instance, the length of Thor's hammer handle would change from moment to moment, ranging from a foot long to croquet-mallet size, and Jack Kirby illustrations would be routinely intercut with panels from Don Heck stories. They used whatever they needed in order to tell the tale. Which of course made no difference to the youngsters watching who couldn't discern between the artists.

In an interview, Grantray-Lawrence President Ray Patterson described the animation process thusly: "We were fortunate to have such fantastic artwork to work with. In blowing up these drawings to 18 by 14 in order to do touchups on them, we found very little that our artists had to tinker with. The animation studio added lip movement here, a raised eyebrow there, and an occasional sweeping arm or leg. Let's face it, the comic book created the illusion of movement very successfully. We merely helped it along a little."

Nowadays the cartoons are mostly remembered for the insidiously catchy theme songs. Composed by Jack Urbont, fans can sing them to this day. In fact, Urbont sued rapper Ghostface Killah for sampling Urbont's Iron Man theme in two songs on the 2000 album *Supreme Clientele*. Iron Man's theme was actually present briefly in the film *Iron Man*: Rhodey's phone plays it as a ring tone when Tony calls him. It's not hard to see why. What other theme song composer would even think of rhyming "gamma rays" with "unglamor-ays"?

THE AVENGERS: EARTH'S MIGHTIEST HEROES

The new animated series debuted on Disney XD in 2010 and embraced the slogan of "Earth's Mightiest Heroes," which had been around since the team's very first issue.

As anyone could have predicted, Loki was once again responsible for assembling the team when he masterminded a simultaneous breakout of villains from various Marvel prisons including the Big House, the Cube, the Raft, and the Vault. The situation required the immediate gathering of a crew that looked very much like the original team: Ant-Man, the Hulk, Thor, and the Wasp, with Iron Man as the team's leader.

ABOVE: From *The Avengers: Earth's Mightiest Heroes* title sequence, showing the whole gang: Hawkeye, Hulk, Cap, Iron Man, Giant Man, Wasp, Thor, and Black Panther.

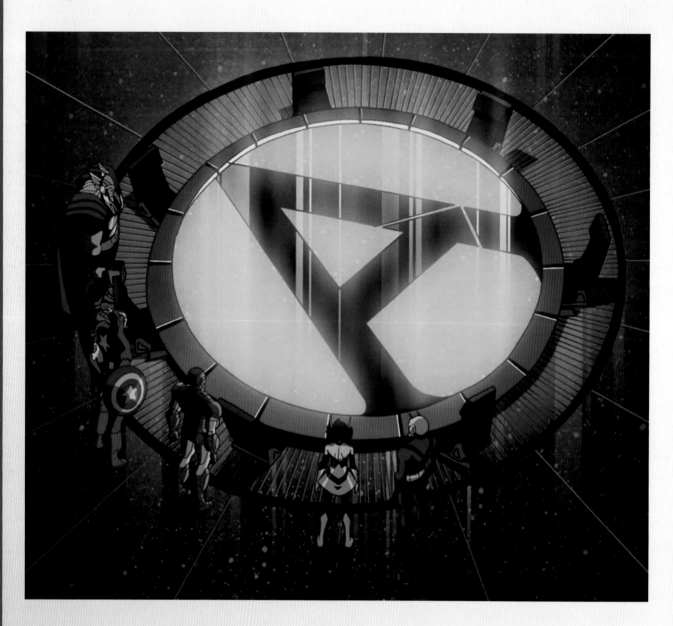

By episode nine, "Living Legend," Captain America had been defrosted and joined up as well.

By the end of the first season, however, unbeknownst to the team, Cap had been replaced by a Skrull—a precursor to the Skrull invasion coming in the second season. Season Two had the crew battling not only the Skrull but also the Kree and eventually, because the series went totally cosmic, Galactus himself.

The series ran for a total of fifty-two well-received episodes.

Story editor Christopher Yost has very vivid recollections of his time on the series:

ABOVE: The number of heroes around the table has grown, as seen in this shot from *The Avengers: Earth's Mightiest Heroes.*

"[Junior Executive Josh Fine] called me up and said, hey—do you want to work on Avengers? Of course I did.

"But unlike the *Fantastic Four*, which the network really wanted to be a comedy, and *Iron Man*, where they wanted Tony Stark to be a teenager, there were no real restrictions here. It was literally just me putting forward what I thought *Avengers* was, my kind of ideal version . . . For more or less fifty-two episodes, we tried to put forward the Avengers that I grew up with, to varying degrees of success. And I'm insanely proud of what we accomplished."

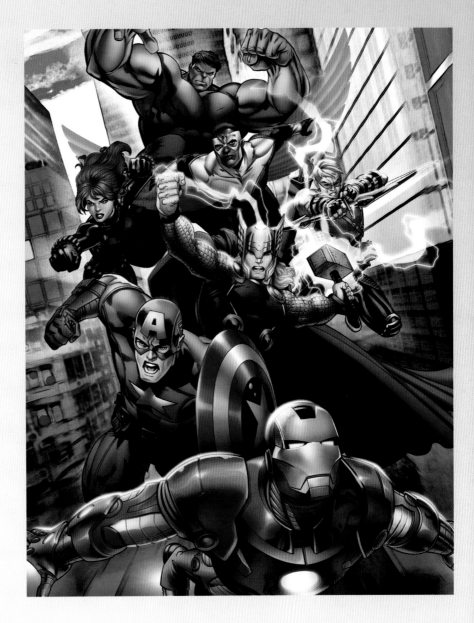

AVENGERS ASSEMBLE

Marvel began a new animated series focusing on the individuals who were spotlighted in the Avengers film. They added a point-of-view character: the Falcon. Serving as the eyes and ears of the audience, the Falcon joins a team composed of Iron Man, Captain America, the Hulk, Black Widow, and Hawkeye. They spend their time going up against a cabal of super villains headed up by the Red Skull.

Avengers Assemble is run by the creative team collectively known as Man of

ABOVE: Hulk, Black Widow, Falcon, Hawkeye, Thor, Cap, and Iron Man.

Action. Composed of Joe Casey, Joe Kelly, Duncan Rouleu, and Steven T. Seagle, Man of Action had earlier gained a name for itself by creating such still-popular series as *Ben 10*.

With a different voice cast from the previous animated series, it debuted in May 2013 on Disney XD. The first season ran twenty-six episodes and by the end was renewed for a second season.

FINAL VIEW

The Avengers always have, and always will be, the centerpiece of the Marvel

ABOVE: Hawkeye, Falcon, Iron Man, Cap, Hulk, and Thor in *Avengers Assemble*.

Universe. Yes, the mutants are popular, and yes, Spider-Man remains the flagship character. But Spider-Man is now a member of the Avengers and was fighting by Captain America's side during the Marvel Civil War. And the events that took place after the return of the Phoenix force resulted in more mutants being eagerly incorporated into the Avengers' ranks. Sooner or later, matters always return to the Avengers.

APPENDIX: COMPLETE AVENGERS ROSTER

FOUNDING MEMBERS

Ant-Man (Hank Pym)

Hulk (Robert Bruce Banner)

Iron Man (Tony Stark)

Thor

Wasp (Janet Van Dyne)

Two-Gun Kid (Matthew "Matt" J.
Hawkins, formerly Matthew Liebowicz)

Captain Marvel (Carol Danvers)

Falcon (Samuel "Snap" Thomas Wilson)

Tigra (Greer Grant Nelson)

She-Hulk (Jennifer Susan Walters)

AVENGERS IN ORDER OF ACCEPTANCE

Captain America

Wonder Man (Simon Williams)

Hawkeye (Clint Barton)

Quicksilver (Pietro Django Maximoff)

Scarlet Witch (Wanda Maximoff)

Swordsman (Jacques Duquesne)

Hercules

Black Panther (T'Challa)

Vision

Black Knight (Dane Whitman)

Black Widow (Natalia Alianovna
Romanova)

Mantis

Beast (Dr. Henry "Hank" McCoy)

Moondragon (Heather Douglas)

Hellcat (Patricia "Patsy" Walker)

BLACK PANTHER

Captain Marvel (Monica Rambeau)

Starfox (Eros)

Sub-Mariner (Namor)

Doctor Druid (Dr. Anthony Ludgate Druid)

Demolition Man (Dennis Dunphy)

Forgotten One (Gilgamesh)

Mr. Fantastic (Reed Richards)

Invisible Woman (Susan Richards, née Storm)

Quasar (Wendell Elvis Vaughn)

Human Torch (Jim Hammond)

Sersi

Stingray (Walter Newell)

Spider-Man (Peter Benjamin Parker)

Sandman (William Baker a.k.a. Flint Marko)

Rage (Elvin Daryl Haliday)

Machine Man (X-51, Aaron Stack)

Living Lightning (Miguel Santos)

Spider-Woman (Julia Carpenter)

Crystal (Crystal Amaquelin Maximoff)

Thunderstrike (Eric Kevin Masterson)

Justice (Vance Astrovik)

Firestar (Angelica Jones)

Triathlon (a.k.a. 3-D Man, Delroy Garrett)

Silverclaw (Maria de Guadalupe Santiago)

Jack of Hearts (Jack Hart)

Ant-Man (Scott Edward Harris Lang)

Captain Britain (a.k.a. Lionheart of Avalon, Kelsey Leigh Shorr)

Luke Cage (a.k.a. Power Man: Carl Lucas [birth name], Lucas Cage [legal name])

Wolverine (James "Logan" Howlett)

Sentry (Robert Reynolds)

Echo (a.k.a. Ronin, Maya Lopez)

THE ILLUMINATI

Black Bolt

Black Panther

Captain America (Steve Rodgers)

Doctor Strange

Iron Man

Mister Fantastic

Namor

Maximus

Hulk

Beast

SPIDER-WOMAN

NEW AVENGERS

Luke Cage

Spider-Man

Wolverine

Sentry

Echo a.k.a. Ronin

Spider-Woman

Iron Fist

Ronin a.k.a Hawkeye, Goliath (Clinton Barton)

Captain America (James Buchanan "Bucky" Barnes)

Mockingbird

Captain Marvel (formerly Binary, Warbird, Ms. Marvel)

Ether Jewel a.k.a. Jessica Jones

Thing

Daredevil

MIGHTY AVENGERS

Current Members:

Luke Cage

Spectrum (previously known as Photon)

Ronin

IRON FIST

Blue Marvel

Power Man

White Tiger

Falcon

She-Hulk (legal council)

Former Members:

Superior Spider-man

Iron Man

Ms. Marvel

Wonder Man (Simon Williams)

The Wasp (Dr. Henry Jonathan "Hank"
Pym)

Black Widow (Natalia Alianovna Romanova
a.k.a Natasha Romanoff)

Sentry

Ares

Spider-Woman

Hercules

Amadeus Cho

Jocasta

U.S. Agent

Stature

Vision II

Quicksilver

Scarlet Witch

WEST COAST AVENGERS

Hawkeye

Mockingbird (Barbara Barton, née Morse)

War Machine (James Rupert "Rhodey"
Rhodes)

Thing (Benjamin Jacob Grimm)

Moon Knight (Marc Spector)

Firebird (Bonita Juárez)

U.S. Agent (John Frank Walker, Jack
Daniels)

Darkhawk (Christopher Powell)

GREAT LAKES AVENGERS

Mr. Immortal (Craig Hollis)

Dinah Soar

Big Bertha (Ashley Crawford)

Flatman (Dr. Val Ventura)

Doorman (DeMarr Davis)

Squirrel Girl (Doreen Green)

Grasshopper

Deadpool (Wade Wilson)

Gravity (Greg Willis)

BLACK WIDOW

ACKNOWLEDGMENTS

Special thanks to Roy Thomas, Will Murray, Chris Boyko, Scott Edelman, Mike Burkey (www.romitaman.com), Kwan Chang, and Heritage Auctions for their assistance with research and obtaining images of original memorabilia for this project. Thank you to Tyler Freidenreich for research assistance.

IMAGE CREDITS

ABOUT THE AUTHOR

Peter A. David is a prolific author whose career spans nearly two decades. He has worked in every conceivable media: television, film, books (fiction, nonfiction, and audio), short stories, and comic books, and acquired followings in all of them.

In the literary field, David has published over a hundred novels, including numerous appearances on the *New York Times* Best Sellers List. His novels include *Artful*, *Sir Apropos of Nothing*, *Knight Life*, *Howling Mad*, and the *Psi-Man* adventure series. He is the cocreator and author of the best-selling *Star Trek: New Frontier* series for Pocket Books, and has also written such Trek novels as *Q-Squared*, *The Siege*, *Q-in-Law*, *Vendetta*, *I, Q* (with John de Lancie), *A Rock and a Hard Place* and *Imzadi*, among others.

David's comic-book resume includes an award-winning twelve-year run on *The Incredible Hulk*, and he has also worked on such varied and popular titles as *X-Factor*, *Friendly Neighborhood Spider-Man*, *Fallen Angel*, *Supergirl*, *Young Justice*, *Soulsearchers and Company*, *Aquaman*, *Spider-Man*, *Spider-Man 2099*, *Star Trek*, *Wolverine*, *The Phantom*, *Sachs & Violens*, and many others. He has also written comic-book related novels, such as *The Hulk: What Savage Beast*, and coedited *The Ultimate Hulk* short story collection. Furthermore, his opinion column *But I Digress* has been running in the industry trade newspaper *The Comic Buyers' Guide* for over a decade.

David is the cocreator, with popular science fiction icon Bill Mumy (of *Lost in Space* and *Babylon 5* fame), of the Cable Ace Award-nominated science fiction series *Space Cases*, which ran for two seasons on Nickelodeon. He has written several scripts for the Hugo Award winning TV series *Babylon 5*, and the sequel series, *Crusade*.

He lives in New York with his wife, Kathleen, and his four children, Shana, Gwen, Ariel, and Caroline.

Published in Great Britain
2015 by Aurum Press Ltd
74–77 White Lion Street
London N1 9PF
www.aurumpress.co.uk

A catalogue record for this book is available from the British Library.

ISBN: 978-1-78131-398-5

Marvel The Avengers Vault is produced by becker&mayer! LLC
Bellevue, Washington
www.beckermayer.com

Designer: Katie Benezra
Editor: Dana Youlin
Photo researcher: Emily Zach
Production coordinator: Tom Miller

Printed and bound in China
10 9 8 7 6 5 4 3 2 1
2019 2018 2017 2016 2015
Project #14270